TO ENGLISH 1

Protase E. Woodford
Doris Kernan

McGRAW-HILL

MÉXICO • BOGOTÁ • BUENOS AIRES • CARACAS • GUATEMALA • LISBOA
MADRID • NUEVA YORK • PANAMÁ • SAN JUAN • SANTIAGO • SÃO PAULO
AUCKLAND • HAMBURGO • LONDRES • MILÁN • MONTREAL • NUEVA DELHI
PARÍS • SAN FRANCISCO • SINGAPUR • ST. LOUIS
SIDNEY • TOKIO • TORONTO

Credits

Editorial Development: Jacqueline Rebisz and Theresa Chimienti
Design: Catherine Gallagher
Copy Editing: Suzanne Shetler
Production: Robert Pedersen
Illustrations: Carolyn Stevenson
Photo Research: Alan Forman

Photo Credits

The authors are indebted to the following persons and organizations for permission to include the following photographs: Pages 2, 4, 8, 10, 43, 46, 49, 70, 74–75, 77, 84, 114, 117: Laimute E. Druskis; 22, 27, 29, 32: Eric Kroll/Taurus Photo; 30: NCR Corporation; 38, 45: U. S. Department of Housing and Urban Development; 54, 59, 61: Arthur Lavine/Chase Manhattan Bank; 63: Citibank; 78, 88–89, 91, 92: Port Authority of New York and New Jersey; 98, 102, 105, 108, 111: U.S. Postal Service. The cover photograph is from Photo Researchers, Inc.

Library of Congress Cataloging in Publication Data

Woodford, Protase E
  Bridges to English.

  1. English language—Text-books for foreigners.
I. Kernan, Doris, joint author. II. Title.
PE1128.W758   428.2′4   80-21012
ISBN 0-07-034481-7 (v. 1)

Bridges to English is a fully articulated series of six English language learning texts designed for the adult student whose first language is other than English. Educational, business, and professional demands, as well as cultural interests, continually force today's adult beyond national boundaries only to find that a sound working knowledge of English is indispensable. To this learner *Bridges to English* is directed.

The principal goal of the study of English is to be able to understand spoken and written English and to make oneself understood. *Bridges to English* is designed to ensure rapid acquisition of the listening, speaking, reading and writing skills necessary for effective communication. The introduction of language constructions, vocabulary, and pronunciation is carefully sequenced and controlled in order to promote efficient patterns of learning through constant reinforcement and extension of skills.

Each lesson integrates development of the listening, speaking, reading and writing skills. The lessons are organized according to the following plan:

New Words   The lesson begins with the new words which are presented in the context of sentences. Sometimes the new words are defined using vocabulary already learned. The questions and brief drills that immediately follow provide the practice which helps to make the new words an active part of the student's vocabulary.

Structure   The structure concepts of each lesson are presented by means of pattern drills. Through a varied series of oral exercises, the student has ample opportunity to learn the grammatical generalizations. A summary of each new structure item follows the oral exercises. After the summary, writing practice which focuses on the new structure concept is provided.

Conversation   The conversation contains previously learned vocabulary and structure. It is designed to be learned with a minimum of effort. The conversation is based on a familiar situation so that the student can immediately talk about the particular situation. Unfamiliar structures are avoided. The questions which follow each conversation serve to check comprehension and permit the learner to use the vocabulary and structures of the conversation. The personal questions encourage the students to apply the situation of the conversation to their own lives.

Reading   The reading selection in each lesson allows the student to apply the newly acquired vocabulary and structure skills. It also serves to review and reinforce language skills learned in preceding lessons. A list of questions follows each reading selection, encouraging the student to discuss the material which has been read.

Lesson Review   Each new language concept is represented in the lesson review. The student is provided a variety of written practice drills in order to promote mastery of the vocabulary and structure items presented in the lesson.

Oral Review   The focus of the oral review is an illustration at the conclusion of each lesson. It serves as a stimulus for oral and written expression, requiring the utilization of the material presented in the lesson.

ABOUT THE AUTHORS

Protase E. Woodford is Associate Director, International Office, Educational Testing Service, Princeton, New Jersey. Formerly he was Director of Language Programs at ETS with responsibility for many language tests, including the TOEFL. He has had extensive language teaching experience at the secondary and college levels and has taught methods at the University of Texas. He has developed an English testing program sponsored by the government of Japan for Japanese business personnel. He has worked extensively with Latin American ministries of education in the area of tests and measurements. He has also worked with the British Council and the English-Speaking Union in developing common descriptors of English language ability. Mr. Woodford has given numerous speeches on language teaching methodology in Europe, Asia, Latin America, Canada, and the United States. He is the author of several language textbooks.

Doris Kernan is presently a Learning Consultant for the South Orange/ Maplewood, New Jersey, Public Schools. Ms. Kernan has taught at all levels of instruction from the elementary to the college level. She has lectured on language teaching methodology and learning psychology in the United States, Europe, Canada, Central America, and Africa. Ms. Kernan is the author of several books for the teaching of English.

TABLE OF CONTENTS _____

TO ENGLISH 1

LESSON 1

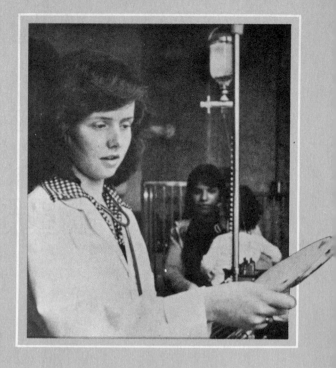

NEW WORDS

1   Ann Ross is a woman.
She's a nurse.
She's American.
The hospital is in the city.
Mrs. Ross is in the hospital.

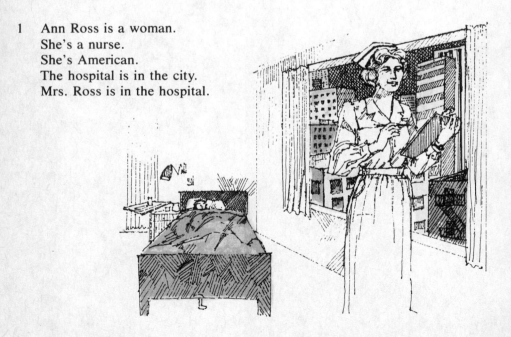

2 John Ross is a man.
   He's a teacher.
   He's American.
   The school is in the country.
   It's not in the city.
   Mr. Ross is in school.

3 Luke and Sara Peters are
     husband and wife.
   They're husband and wife.
   The store is small.
   It's not big.
   Mr. and Mrs. Peters are in the
     store.

A Answer the questions.

1 Is Ann Ross a nurse?
2 What is she?
3 Is she American?
4 Is the hospital in the city?
5 Where is the hospital?
6 Is Mrs. Ross in the hospital?
7 Who is in the hospital?
8 Is John Ross a teacher?
9 What is he?
10 Is he American?
11 Is the school in the country?
12 Is the school in the city?
13 Is Mr. Ross in school?
14 Who is in school?
15 Are Luke and Sara Peters husband and wife?
16 Are they husband and wife?
17 Is the store small?
18 Is it big?
19 Are Mr. and Mrs. Peters in the store?

The man and woman are husband and wife.

B Ask questions. Use *who, where,* or *what.*

Mrs. *Gordon* is in the store. →
Who is in the store?

1 *Mr. Ross* is in school.
2 Mrs. Peters is *a nurse.*
3 The nurse is *in the hospital.*
4 *Mr. Peters* is American.
5 *Mrs. Gordon* is in the city.
6 She's *a teacher.*
7 He's *in the store.*
8 The hospital is *in the country.*
9 Mrs. Peters and Mr. Gordon are *in the city.*
10 He's *a teacher.*

MORE NEW WORDS

banker

student

boy

doctor

house

girl

lawyer

Verb *to be*

She is, he is, it is

A Repeat.
Mrs. Ross is a nurse.
Mr. Ross is a teacher.
The school is small.

B Answer.
Is Mrs. Ross a nurse?
Is Mrs. Ross in the hospital?
Is Mrs. Ross American?
What is Mrs. Ross?
Who is in the hospital?
Where is Mrs. Ross?
Is Mr. Ross a teacher?
Is Mr. Ross in school?
Is Mr. Ross American?
What is Mr. Ross?
Who is in school?
Where is Mr. Ross?
Is the school small?
Is the school in the country?
Where is the school?

C Repeat.
Mrs. Gordon is a doctor.
She is a doctor.
She's a doctor.

Mr. Peters is a lawyer.
He is a lawyer.
He's a lawyer.

The store is in the city.
It is in the city.
It's in the city.

D Answer. Use *he's*, *she's*, or *it's*.

Is Mrs. Ross a nurse? →
Yes, she's a nurse.

Is Mrs. Blake a nurse?
Is she American?
Is she in the city?

Is Mr. Gordon a lawyer?
Is he American?
Is he in the country?
Is the house big?
Is it in the city?
Is the store small?
Is it in the country?

I am

A   Repeat.
I am a student.
I'm a student.
I'm in school.

B   Answer. Use *I'm*.
Are you a student?
Are you a teacher or a student?
What are you?
Are you in school?
Are you in the city?
Where are you?
Are you Mr. (Mrs.) _____?
Who are you?
Are you a man or a woman?
Are you in the country or in the city?

You are, we are, they are

A   Repeat.
You are a teacher.
You're a teacher.
You and Mr. (Mrs.) _____ are in school.

B   Follow the model.

> Who is a student? →
> You're a student.

Who is a nurse?
Who is in the country?
Who is in the house?
Who is a doctor?
Who is a lawyer?
Who is in the city?
Who is in school?
Who is a student?
Who is Mr. (Mrs.) _____?

C **Repeat.**
Mr. Ross and I are in school.
We are in school.
We're in school.

D **Answer. Use** *we're.*
Are you and Mr. Peters in the city?
Are you and Mrs. Ross in the store?
Are you in school?
Are you in the country?
Are you in the city?
Are you in the hospital in the city?
Are you in the house in the country?
Where are you?

E **Repeat.**
Mr. and Mrs. Ross are husband and wife.
They are husband and wife.
They're in the house.

F **Answer. Use** *they're.*
Are Mr. and Mrs. Gordon in the store?
Are Mr. Ross and Mrs. Peters in school?
Are they in the city?
Are they in the hospital?
Are they in the house?
Are they in the country?
Are they in the hospital in the city?
Where are they?

Mr. Crane is a teacher.

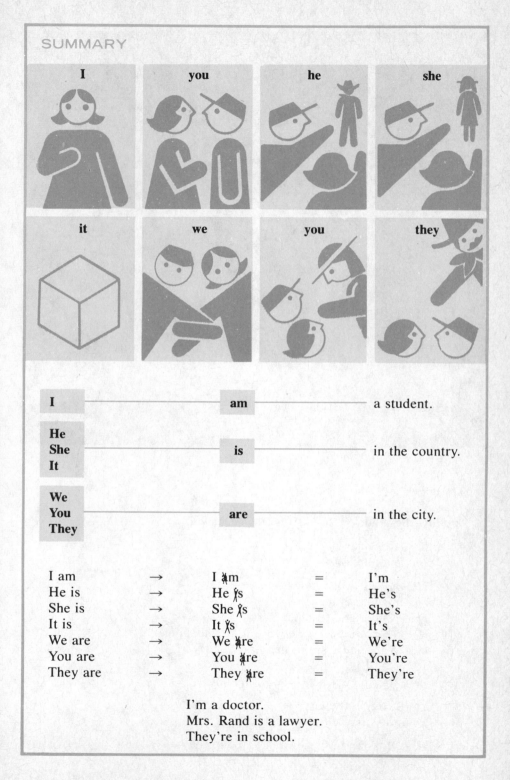

I	**am**	a student.
He **She** **It**	**is**	in the country.
We **You** **They**	**are**	in the city.

I am	→	I am	=	I'm
He is	→	He is	=	He's
She is	→	She is	=	She's
It is	→	It is	=	It's
We are	→	We are	=	We're
You are	→	You are	=	You're
They are	→	They are	=	They're

I'm a doctor.
Mrs. Rand is a lawyer.
They're in school.

Writing Practice

A Follow the model: Use *he, she, it, we,* or *they.*

> *Mrs. Ross* is a nurse. →
> *She* is a nurse.

1 *The man* is in the house.
2 *The hospital* is big.
3 *The woman* is a teacher.
4 *Mr. Peters and Mrs. Day* are in the hospital.
5 *Mrs. Ross and I* are in the store.

B Complete the sentences. Use *am, are,* or *is.*

> You _____ in the city. →
> You are in the city.

1 Mrs. Ross and Mr. Gordon _____ in the house.
2 The store _____ big.

3 We _____ in school.
4 They _____ husband and wife.
5 I _____ a lawyer.
6 I _____ Mr. Jones.
7 Mr. Jones _____ a teacher in the country.
8 Mrs. Allen _____ a lawyer.
9 It _____ a big school.
10 You _____ in school.

C Follow the model. Use *I'm, he's, she's, it's, we're, you're, they're*.

   Is Mrs. May a teacher? →
   Yes, she's a teacher.

1 Are you a student?
2 Is Mr. Dyer a lawyer?
3 Is the store big?
4 Are Mr. and Mrs. Hill in the city?
5 Are you and I in school?
6 Is Mrs. Ross in the hospital?
7 Am I a teacher?

Negative *not*

A **Repeat.**
The house is small.
The house is not big.

We're in the store.
We're not in the house.

I'm a teacher.
I'm not a student.

B **Follow the model. Use *not*.**

   I'm Mrs. Day. →
   I'm not Mrs. Day.

She's a student.
The hospital is big.
The doctor is in the hospital.
You're in school.
Mrs. Gordon and I are in the store.
We're in the city.
They're in the country.
I'm American.
I'm a teacher.

C Answer. Use *not*.

Is the school in the city? →
No, it's not in the city.

Is Mr. Gordon a doctor?
Is he a lawyer?
Is the house in the country?
Is it small?
Are you and Mrs. Gordon in school?
Are you in the store?
Are you in the city?
Are Mr. and Mrs. Peters in the house?
Are they in the hospital?
Are they in the country?
Are you American?
Are you a teacher?

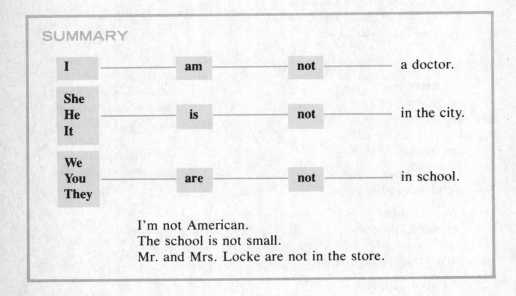

SUMMARY

I	am	not	a doctor.
She He It	is	not	in the city.
We You They	are	not	in school.

I'm not American.
The school is not small.
Mr. and Mrs. Locke are not in the store.

Writing Practice

Answer the questions. Use *not*.

Are you a lawyer? →
No, I'm not a lawyer.

1   Are you American?
2   Is Mr. Peters a banker?
3   Is Mrs. Ross a doctor?
4   Am I a teacher?

5 Are we in school?
6 Is the teacher in the city?
7 Are Mr. Ross and Mrs. Peters in the country?
8 Is the doctor in the hospital?
9 Is the school in the country?
10 Are Mr. and Mrs. Craig American?

Short answers with *to be*

Yes

A Repeat.
Is he a doctor? Yes, he is.
Is Mrs. Ross a nurse? Yes, she is.
Is the school big? Yes, it is.
Are you a nurse? Yes, I am.
Am I a teacher? Yes, you are.
Are you and Mrs. Miller in school? Yes, we are.
Are they in the city? Yes, they are.

B Answer. Use *yes* and short answers.
Is Mr. Grant a student?
Is he in school?
Is Mrs. Ross American?
Is she in the house?
Is the school in the city?
Is it big?
Are you a banker?
Are you in the store?
Are you and Mrs. Lee in the hospital?
Are you in the country?
Are James and Laura Clark husband and wife?
Are they American?

No

A Repeat.
Is he a student? No, he's not.
Is Mrs. Clark a doctor? No, she's not.
Is the store small? No, it's not.
Are you a nurse? No, I'm not.
Am I a student? No, you're not.
Are you and the teacher in the hospital? No, we're not.
Are they in school? No, they're not.

B **Answer. Use *no* and short answers.**

Is Mr. Clay in the hospital?
Is he a teacher?
Is the girl in the house?
Is she in school?
Is the house in the country?
Is it small?
Are you a doctor?
Are you American?
Are you and Mr. Hoban in the city?
Are you in the store?
Are the man and woman American?
Are they husband and wife?

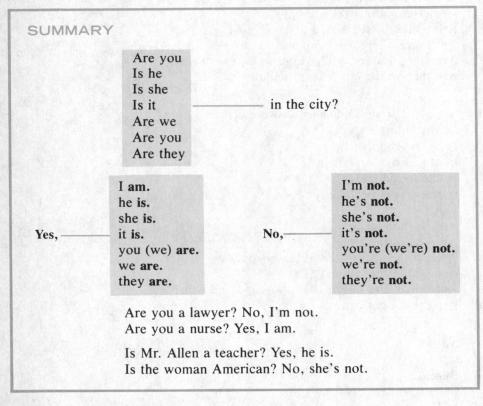

SUMMARY

Are you
Is he
Is she
Is it ———————— in the city?
Are we
Are you
Are they

Yes,——— I am.
he is.
she is.
it is.
you (we) are.
we are.
they are.

No,——— I'm **not**.
he's **not**.
she's **not**.
it's **not**.
you're (we're) **not**.
we're **not**.
they're **not**.

Are you a lawyer? No, I'm not.
Are you a nurse? Yes, I am.

Is Mr. Allen a teacher? Yes, he is.
Is the woman American? No, she's not.

Writing Practice

Write the short answers.

1   Is the house in the city? No, _____.
2   Are Mr. and Mrs. Blake in the hospital? Yes, _____.
3   Are you a student? Yes, _____.

4 Are you a lawyer? No, _____.
5 Is Mrs. Harris a student? Yes, _____.
6 Is Mr. Ross in school? No, _____.
7 Are you and Mrs. Martin American? No, _____.
8 Is the teacher in school? Yes, _____.

Preposition *in*

A Repeat.
They're in the hospital.
The boy is in school.
We're in the country.

B Answer.
Is the man in the house?
Is the girl in the hospital?
Are Mr. and Mrs. Peters in the store?
Is the nurse in the city?
Are you in school?
Are you in the country?
Who is in the hospital?
Who is in school?
Where is the woman (man)?
Where are Mr. and Mrs. Ross?
Where are you?

SUMMARY

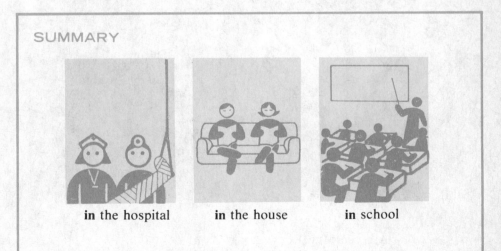

in the hospital   in the house   in school

We're in the city.
The doctor is in the house.
I'm in school.

Answer the questions. Use *in*.

> (store)   Where is the boy? →
> The boy is in the store.

1   (city)   Where is the banker?
2   (school)   Where are you?
3   (hospital)   Where are Mr. and Mrs. Peters?
4   (house)   Where is the man?
5   (store)   Where are you and Mrs. Ross?
6   (country)   Where is the house?
7   (school)   Where is the teacher?
8   (city)   Where are they?

CONVERSATIONS

Who is Mrs. Ross?

Mrs. Gordon	Are you Mrs. Ross?
Mrs. Day	No, I'm not. I'm Mrs. Day.
Mrs. Gordon	Who is Mrs. Ross?
Mrs. Day	She's Mrs. Ross.
Mrs. Gordon	Oh, is she a teacher?
Mrs. Day	No, she's not. She's a nurse.

Questions

1 Is the woman Mrs. Ross?
2 Is she Mrs. Day?
3 Who is Mrs. Ross?
4 Is Mrs. Ross a teacher?
5 Is she a nurse?
6 What is she?

Who is Mr. Gordon?

Mr. Ross   Are you Mr. Gordon?
Mr. Lee   No, I'm not. I'm Mr. Lee.
Mr. Ross   Who is Mr. Gordon?
Mr. Lee   He's Mr. Gordon.
Mr. Ross   Oh, is he a lawyer?
Mr. Lee   No, he's not. He's a teacher.

Questions

1 Is the man Mr. Gordon?
2 Is he Mr. Lee?
3 Who is Mr. Gordon?
4 Is Mr. Gordon a lawyer?
5 Is he a teacher?
6 What is he?

Who are you?

Mr. Johnson	Are you Mr. and Mrs. Peters?
Mrs. Gordon	No, we're not. They're Mr. and Mrs. Peters.
Mrs. Johnson	Who are you?
Mr. Gordon	We're Mr. and Mrs. Gordon.

Questions

1 Are they Mr. and Mrs. Peters?
2 Are they Mr. and Mrs. Gordon?
3 Who are they?

Personal Questions

1 Who are you?
2 Where are you?
3 Are you American?
4 What are you?

Greetings:
Student 1 Hello.
Student 2 Hello.
Student 1 How are you?
Student 2 I'm fine, thanks, and you?
Student 1 Fine, thanks.

READING

Mr. and Mrs. Ross

The man and woman are Mr. and Mrs. Ross. They're husband and wife. They're American. Mrs. Ross is a nurse in a big hospital. The hospital is in the city. Mr. Ross is a teacher in a small school. The school is not in the city. It's in the country.

Questions

1   Are the man and woman Mr. and Mrs. Ross?
2   Who are they?
3   Are they husband and wife?
4   Are they American?
5   What are they?
6   What is Mrs. Ross?
7   Where is she a nurse?
8   Where is the hospital?
9   Is Mr. Ross a teacher?
10   What is he?
11   Where is he a teacher?
12   Is the school in the city?
13   Where is the school?

I Complete the sentences.

It's not big. It's _____. →
It's not big. It's small.

the	is	country	not
hospital	They	I	big
in	Mr.	am	We
Where	Who	What	and
are	school		

1 _____ Gordon is a teacher.
2 The school is in the _____.
3 You _____ a doctor.
4 _____ am a lawyer.
5 I _____ in the house.
6 A city is _____.
7 The banker is in _____ city.
8 _____ is the man? He's in the store.
9 We're _____ in the country. We're in the city.
10 The hospital _____ big.
11 Mr. _____ Mrs. Gordon are husband and wife.
12 _____ is the woman? She's Mrs. Ross.
13 The teacher is in a small _____.
14 I'm a doctor. _____ are you?
15 Who are they? _____'re Mr. and Mrs. Day.
16 Where are you and Mr. Gordon? _____'re in the country.
17 The small school is _____ the country.
18 The nurse is in a big _____.

II Answer the questions. Write a story.

Who are you?
Are you a woman or a man?
Are you American?
Are you a student?
Are you in school?
Is the school big or small?
Is it in the city or in the country?

LESSON 2

1 The man lives in the city.
   He hurries to the telephone.
   He calls a friend.
   The boy studies English.

2   Miss Lyons drives the car.
    She drives with Miss Hunter.
    They leave the city.
    They go to the country.
    It's very hot in the city today.
    It's nice in the country.

3   Mrs. Bell goes to the store
        every day.
    She always buys a newspaper.
    Sometimes she buys a
        magazine too.

4 The girls swim in the lake.
The boy also swims in the lake.
The man reads a magazine.
He sees a picture of a car.
The woman carries a picnic
basket.

A Answer the questions.

1 Where does the man live?
2 Does he hurry to the telephone?
3 Does he call a friend?
4 Who studies English?
5 Who drives the car?
6 Does she drive with Miss Hunter?
7 Do they leave the city?
8 Do they go to the country?
9 Where do they go?
10 Is it very hot in the city today?
11 Is it nice in the country?
12 Does Mrs. Bell go to the store every day?
13 When does she go to the store?
14 Does she always buy a newspaper?
15 What does she always buy?
16 Does she sometimes buy a magazine too?
17 Who swims in the lake?
18 Does the boy also swim in the lake?
19 What does the man read?
20 Does he see a picture of a car?
21 Who carries a picnic basket?

B Complete the sentences.

1 Miss Hunter drives a big ____.
2 They ____ in the lake.

3   They leave the city and drive to the _____.
4   She buys a newspaper in the _____.
5   We swim in the _____ in the country.
6   I hurry to the _____ and call the doctor.
7   It's _____ in the city; it's nice in the country.
8   Do you always buy a magazine and a _____?
9   They read the newspaper every _____.
10 He drives to school with a _____.

MORE NEW WORDS

here   there   book

STRUCTURE

Verbs like *to live*

She lives, he lives

A   Repeat.
She lives in the country.
He reads the newspaper every day.
Mr. Day goes to school in the city.

B   Answer.

Does Miss Hunter live here? →
Yes, Miss Hunter lives here.

Does Miss Lyons drive?
Does she drive every day?
Does she always go to the city?
Does Mr. Gordon live in the country?
Does he leave the country every day?
Does Mrs. Ross go to the store every day?
Does she read a magazine every day?
Does Mr. Peters always buy a newspaper?
Does he read the newspaper every day?

Does the boy carry the newspaper?
Does he study English?
Does he always hurry to school?

I live, you live, we live, they live

A Repeat.

I live in a small house.
You drive a big car.
We swim every day.
They always go to the country.

B Answer. Use *I*.

Do you live in the city?
Do you drive a car?
Do you swim in the lake?
Do you read the newspaper?
Do you go to school?
Do you study every day?

C Answer. Use *we*.

Do you and a friend leave the city?
Do you drive to the country?
Do you hurry to the lake?
Do you swim in the lake?
Do you go to the store every day?
Do you read every day?

D Answer.

Do Mr. and Mrs. Bell read the newspaper every day?
Do they see a picture in the newspaper?
Do they sometimes buy a magazine too?
Do they live in the country?
Do they always see the doctor?
Do they hurry to the city?

E Follow the model.

They drive. →
And you drive too.

They swim every day.
They read the newspaper.
They hurry every day.
They always go to the country.
They live in the city.
They drive a small car.

Do you swim in the lake?

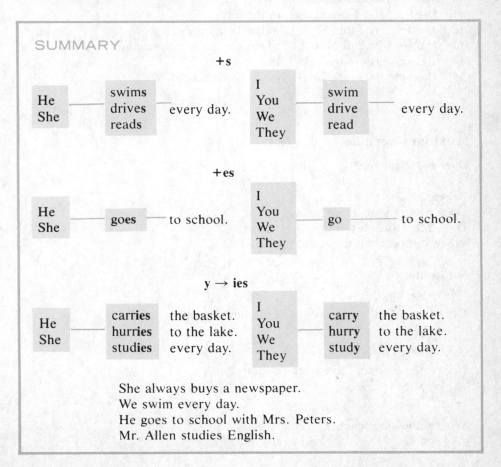

SUMMARY

+s

He She	swims drives reads	every day.

I You We They	swim drive read	every day.

+es

He She	goes	to school.

I You We They	go	to school.

y → ies

He She	carries hurries studies	the basket. to the lake. every day.

I You We They	carry hurry study	the basket. to the lake. every day.

She always buys a newspaper.
We swim every day.
He goes to school with Mrs. Peters.
Mr. Allen studies English.

Follow the models.

> (go)   The man _____ to the lake. →
> The man goes to the lake.
>
> (swim)   You _____ every day. →
> You swim every day.

1   (live)   I _____ in the city.
2   (call)   Mr. and Mrs. Ross _____ a friend.
3   (read)   We _____ the newspaper.
4   (go)   They _____ to the country.
5   (see)   You _____ the picture in the book.
6   (leave)   I _____ the house and go to school.
7   (carry)   She _____ the picnic basket.
8   (go)   Miss Lyons _____ to the store.
9   (read)   Mr. Ross _____ the newspaper every day.
10   (buy)   He also _____ a book.
11   (live)   Miss Crane _____ in the city.
12   (swim)   You and I _____ in the lake every day.
13   (buy)   Mr. and Mrs. Lee always _____ a newspaper.
14   (leave)   The nurse _____ the hospital.
15   (hurry)   Mrs. Blake always _____ to school.

Auxiliary verb *do*

Does he? Does she?

A   Repeat.
Does Miss Lyons drive?
Does Mr. Gordon swim?
When does she go to school?

B   Substitute.

Does | Mr. Peters / the man / he | always read the newspaper?

Does | Mrs. Ross / the woman / she | live in the country?

Where does the teacher | live? / buy the book? / go every day?

C Follow the model. Use *does*.

Mrs. Ross reads a magazine every day. →
Does Mrs. Ross read a magazine every day?

The man buys a newspaper every day.
He swims every day.
The doctor hurries to the hospital every day.
The nurse drives to the city every day.
She goes to the store every day.

D Practice.
Ask if Mr. Gordon swims.
Ask if he drives.
Ask if he lives in the city.
Ask when Mrs. Ross goes to the hospital.
Ask where she sees a picture of the car.
Ask what she buys in the store.

In the country

Do you? Do they?

A Repeat.
Do you read the newspaper?
Do they always call the doctor?
Where do you go to school?
What do they buy in the store?

B Follow the model.

> They drive. →
> Do you drive too?

They swim.
They read.
They study every day.
They drive a small car.
They live in the city.
They go to school.

Does the woman go to the store every day?

C   Follow the model.

> We read every day. →
> Do they read every day too?

We hurry every day.
We swim every day.
We drive every day.
We call the doctor every day.
We go to the store every day.
We buy a newspaper every day.

D   Practice.
Ask a student if she drives to school.
Ask a student if he goes to the country.
Ask a student where he buys the magazine.
Ask a student when she goes to school.

Ask a student if Mr. and Mrs. Ross live in the city.
Ask a student if they read the newspaper every day.
Ask a student when Miss Lyons and Miss Hunter drive to the lake.
Ask a student what they see in the country.

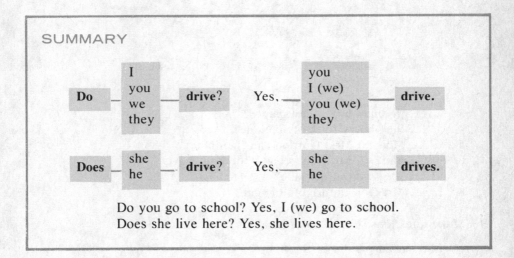

SUMMARY

| Do | I
you
we
they | drive? | Yes, | you
I (we)
you (we)
they | drive. |

| Does | she
he | drive? | Yes, | she
he | drives. |

Do you go to school? Yes, I (we) go to school.
Does she live here? Yes, she lives here.

Writing Practice

A   Complete the questions. Use *do* or *does*.

> _____ the woman swim? →
> Does the woman swim?

1   _____ you live in the city?
2   _____ Miss Hunter drive?

31

It's hot in the city.

3 _____ the man buy a newspaper?
4 _____ they hurry to the telephone?
5 _____ Mr. and Mrs. Gordon call the doctor?
6 _____ you and Mr. Peters leave the house every day?
7 _____ she swim in the lake?
8 _____ Mr. Gordon drive a big car?

B Make questions. Use *do* or *does*.

She sees a picture of the house. →
Does she see a picture of the house?

1 They drive to the city.
2 You hurry to school.
3 She goes to school every day.
4 He swims in the lake.
5 Mr. and Mrs. Ross call the teacher.
6 Miss Lyons leaves the house.
7 You go to the country.
8 They always drive to school.

Preposition *to*

A   Repeat.

Miss Lyons drives to the city.
The man hurries to the telephone.
The students go to school.

B   Answer.

Do you hurry to the store?
Do you drive to the city?
Do you go to the country sometimes?
Does the doctor drive to the hospital?
Does the man go to the store every day?
Does the woman always go to the lake?
Does the teacher go to school every day?

SUMMARY

to the city   **to** the store

I always go to the country.
Do you drive to school every day?

Writing Practice

Make sentences. Use *to*.

she drives / city →
She drives to the city.

1   you go / country
2   Mrs. Ross hurries / lake
3   I drive / hospital
4   he goes / store every day
5   we go / school
6   Mr. and Mrs. Gordon drive / city

CONVERSATION

Do you drive?

Mr. Ames	Do you live here in the city?
Mr. Hart	No, I live in the country.
Mr. Ames	Do you drive to the city every day?
Mr. Hart	Yes, I drive a small car.
Mr. Ames	What about Mr. and Mrs. Carter? Do they drive too?
Mr. Hart	Yes, there they are in the car.
Mr. Ames	Does Mrs. Carter drive?
Mr. Hart	Yes, sometimes she drives and sometimes he drives.

Questions

1   Where does Mr. Hart live?
2   Does he drive to the city every day?
3   Does he drive a small car?
4   Do Mr. and Mrs. Carter drive too?
5   Where are Mr. and Mrs. Carter?
6   Does Mrs. Carter drive?
7   Does Mr. Carter drive sometimes?

Personal Questions

1   Do you live in the city or the country?
2   Where do you go to school?
3   What do you study?

4 Do you carry a book to school?
5 Do you read the book?
6 Does the teacher sometimes read the book?

READING

The city and the country

Miss Lyons lives in a big city. Every day she goes to the store. In the store she always buys a newspaper. Today she also buys a magazine. In the magazine she sees a picture of a lake.

    Miss Lyons leaves the store and hurries to a telephone. She calls a friend, Miss Hunter. Today it's very hot in the city. Miss Lyons and Miss Hunter drive to the country. In the country they go to a lake. They carry a picnic basket and a magazine to the lake. They swim and they read. It's very nice here in the country.

Questions

1 Does Miss Lyons live in a big city?
2 Where does she go every day?
3 What does she always buy in the store?
4 What does she also buy today?
5 What does she see in the magazine?
6 Does Miss Lyons leave the store?
7 Does she hurry to a telephone?

8   Does she call a friend?
9   Who is the friend?
10 Is it very hot in the city today?
11 Do Miss Lyons and Miss Hunter drive to the country?
12 Where do they go?
13 What do they carry to the lake?
14 Do they swim and read?
15 Is it very nice in the country?

LESSON REVIEW

I   Complete the sentences.

She _____ a picture of a car. →
She sees a picture of a car.

swims	too	telephone	leave	hot
newspaper	to	hurries	drives	call
live	buy	go	reads	of

1   They *Live* in a small house.
2   She *drives* to the telephone and calls a friend.
3   It's very *hot* in the city today.
4   I hurry to the *telephone* and call the doctor.
5   The man *swims* in the lake.
6   Miss Lyons *buy* a nice car.
7   You see a telephone. You _____ a friend.
8   The doctor drives _____ the hospital.
9   He sees a picture in the _____.
10   The teacher _____ the book in school.
11–12 We _____ to the store and _____ a newspaper every day.
13   I always read the newspaper. Today I read a magazine _____.
14   They _____ the house and drive to the city.
15   Do you see a picture _____ the house in the newspaper?

II Answer the questions. Write a story.

Do you live in the city?
Do you go to the store every day?
Do you always buy a newspaper in the store?
Do you sometimes buy a magazine?
Do you also buy a magazine today?
Do you see a picture in the magazine?
Is it a picture of a lake?
Is the lake in the country?
Do you drive to the country with a friend?
Do you swim in the lake?
Is it nice in the country?

LESSON 3

NEW WORDS

1 The Davis family is in the house now.
Mr. Davis is the father.
Mrs. Davis is the mother.
They have two sons and two daughters.

2   The newspaper is near the
        door.
    Every morning Mrs. Davis
        finds the newspaper there.
    Mrs. Davis lives in a quiet
        neighborhood.

3   The house is near a park.
    The house is for sale.
    The kitchen and the living
        room are downstairs.
    The bedrooms and the
        bathroom are upstairs.
    The house has many rooms.
    It has a small yard.
    It doesn't have a garage,
        though.
    Mr. and Mrs. Bell don't buy
        the house.

4   The car is old.
    Mr. and Mrs. Adams have to
       buy a new car.
    They see a car.
    It's not expensive.
    They're happy with the price.

A Answer the questions.

1   Is the Davis family in the house now?
2   Who is the father?
3   Who is the mother?
4   Do they have two sons and two daughters?
5   How many sons and daughters do they have?
6   Where is the newspaper?
7   Who finds the newspaper there every morning?
8   Does Mrs. Davis live in a quiet neighborhood?
9   Is the house near a park?
10 Is the house for sale?
11 Where is the kitchen?
12 Where is the living room?
13 Where are the bedrooms and the bathroom?
14 Does the house have many rooms?
15 Does it have a small yard?
16 Does the house have a garage?
17 Do Mr. and Mrs. Bell buy the house?
18 Is the car old?
19 Do Mr. and Mrs. Adams have to buy a new car?
20 Do they see a car?
21 Is it expensive?
22 Are they happy with the price?

B Follow the model.

   big → small

   1 new   5 woman
   2 big   6 teacher
   3 upstairs   7 wife
   4 boy

MORE NEW WORDS

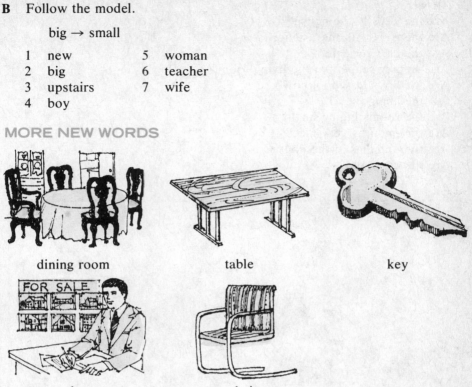

   dining room   table   key

   realtor   chair

STRUCTURE

Noun plurals: *key/keys*

A **Repeat.**
   The girls are in school.
   The newspapers are for sale.
   The keys are in the car.
   Many families live here.

B **Substitute.**

                    newspapers
   She buys two   pictures   in the store.
                    chairs

            doctors
   The   lawyers   are not in the city.
            teachers

C Answer.
Are the keys in the house?
Are the girls with the teacher?
Are the cars for sale?
Are the newspapers in the living room?
Are the boys in school now?
Are the chairs new?
Are the rooms big or small?
Are the pictures very nice?
Are two families in the house?
Are the cities old?

SUMMARY

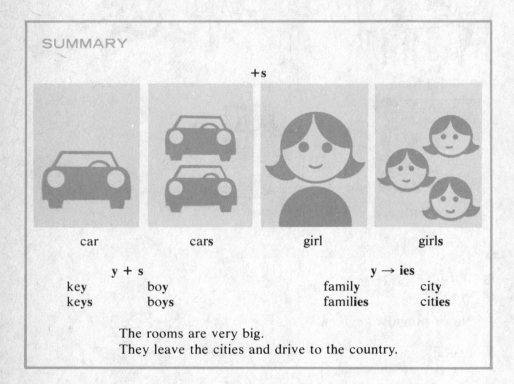

+s

car   cars   girl   girls

y + s   y → ies
key   boy   family   city
keys   boys   families   cities

The rooms are very big.
They leave the cities and drive to the country.

Writing Practice

Make the words plural. Follow the model.

(car) She sees the _____. →
She sees the cars.

1 (girl) The nurse calls the _____.
2 (teacher) Many _____ live near the school.
3 (store) The school is near many _____.

Where is the family?

4 (picture) I see the _____ in the book.
5 (key) The _____ are not in the house.
6 (boy) The _____ leave in the morning.
7 (bedroom) The _____ are upstairs.
8 (newspaper) Mrs. Johnson reads many _____.
9 (city) Tokyo and New York are big _____.
10 (family) Many _____ drive to the lake.

Verb *to have*

She has, he has, it has

A Repeat.
Mrs. Davis has a new car.
Mr. Allen has two sons.
The house has six rooms.

B Answer.
Does the woman have a big family?
Does Mrs. Ross have a son?
Does she have a new car?
Does the man have a big house?
Does Mr. Davis have a house near the lake?
Does he have a garage?
Does the house have many rooms?
Does it have a dining room?
Does it have three bedrooms too?

I have, you have, we have, they have

A Repeat.
I have a new car.
You have a nice house.
We have two telephones.
They have the keys.

B Answer. Use *I*.
Do you have the keys?
Do you have the magazine?
Do you have a house in the country?
Do you have a big bedroom?
Do you have a small family?

C Answer. Use *we*.
Do you and Mrs. Davis have a son?
Do you have a daughter too?
Do you have a new car?
Do you have a house for sale?
Do you have a telephone in the house?

D Answer.
Do Mr. and Mrs. Ross have a daughter?
Do they have a car for sale?
Do they have many friends?
Do they have a dining room in the house?
Do they have chairs in the room?

E Follow the model.

Who has a son? →
You have a son.

Who has a small car?
Who has a new house?

Who has a big family?
Who has a newspaper?
Who has a house in the country?

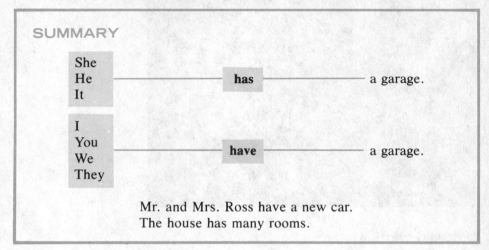

SUMMARY

She He It	has	a garage.
I You We They	have	a garage.

Mr. and Mrs. Ross have a new car.
The house has many rooms.

Does the house have a garage?

45

In the kitchen

Writing Practice

Complete the sentences. Use *have* or *has*.

The girl _____ the keys. →
The girl has the keys.

1 You _____ the magazine.
2 They _____ many rooms in the house.
3 I _____ a house for sale.
4 We _____ a big car.
5 Mrs. Ross _____ a telephone in the kitchen.
6 Mr. Gordon _____ two sons.
7 You and I _____ a big bedroom.
8 The doctors _____ the keys.
9 The house _____ many rooms.
10 The house _____ a new garage.

To have to

A **Repeat.**
She has to go to the doctor.
I have to buy a book.
You have to find the house.
We have to leave now.

B **Answer.**
Does the girl have to go to school?
Does she have to leave now?
Does the man have to hurry every day?

46

Do I have to call the doctor?
Do I have to leave in the morning?
Do you have to go now?
Do you have to buy a new car?
Do you and Miss Penn have to go to the hospital?
Do the boys have to read the book?
Do they have to call the teacher?

SUMMARY

| He / She | — **has to** — | go to the doctor. |

| I / You / We / They | — **have to** — | go to school. |

When do you have to leave?
She has to go now.

Writing Practice

Complete the sentences. Use *have to* or *has to*.

1 I _____ see the doctor today.
2 He _____ drive to the city every day.
3 We _____ buy a new house.
4 You _____ go to school.
5 The woman _____ leave in the morning.
6 I _____ call the nurse.
7 You and Mrs. Sands _____ go to the hospital.
8 You and I _____ find the keys.
9 Father _____ see the doctor.
10 The bankers _____ live in the city.

Negative *not* with regular verbs

A Repeat.
The girl reads the magazine.
The girl doesn't read the book.

I live in the country.
I don't live in the city.

B Substitute.

Mr. Carr doesn't {swim. / drive. / see.}

I / You / We / They don't have a car.

C Answer. Use *doesn't* or *don't*.

Do you drive to school? →
No, I don't drive to school.

Does the woman buy a newspaper every day?
Does the boy hurry to school?
Does the banker call the lawyer?
Does Miss Lyons swim?
Does she go to school?
Does the house have a garage?
Does it have two bathrooms?
Do you live in the country?
Do you have the newspaper?
Do Mr. and Mrs. Peters drive every day?
Do they go to the city?
Do we have to leave now?
Do we study every day?

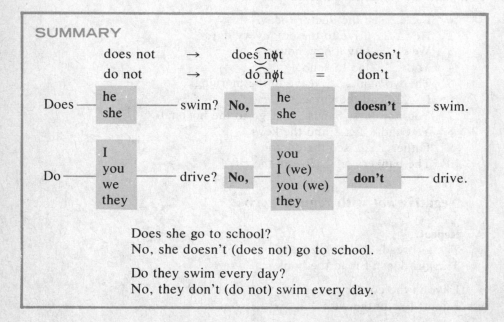

SUMMARY

does not → does nøt = doesn't
do not → do nøt = don't

Does — he / she — swim? **No,** — he / she — **doesn't** — swim.

Do — I / you / we / they — drive? **No,** — you / I (we) / you (we) / they — **don't** — drive.

Does she go to school?
No, she doesn't (does not) go to school.

Do they swim every day?
No, they don't (do not) swim every day.

Writing Practice

A Complete the sentences. Use *doesn't* or *don't*.

> Mr. Allen ____ drive. →
> Mr. Allen doesn't drive.

1 Miss Stone ____ read the newspaper.
2 I ____ live in a big house.
3 Mr. Baines ____ go to school in the city.
4 He ____ have a car.
5 We ____ always hurry to school.
6 You ____ study every day.
7 Mr. and Mrs. Peters ____ have to study today.
8 They ____ buy magazines.

B Answer the questions. Use *doesn't* or *don't*.

> Do you swim? →
> No, I don't swim.

1 Does she drive every day?
2 Do they always go to the country?
3 Does he live in the city?
4 Do you read the newspaper every day?
5 Does Miss Hunter have a car?
6 Do you and Mrs. Peters go to the store every day?
7 Do I have to leave now?
8 Does the house have a big yard?

In the living room

CONVERSATION

House for sale

Realtor	Morgan Realty. Good morning.
Mrs. Nolan	Good morning. I'm Mrs. Nolan. I see in the newspaper you have a house for sale.
Realtor	Yes, it's a very nice house in a quiet neighborhood.
Mrs. Nolan	We have two sons and two daughters, so we have to buy a big house. How many bedrooms does the house have?
Realtor	It has three bedrooms. It also has a living room, a bathroom, and a new kitchen. It doesn't have a garage, though.
Mrs. Nolan	Oh, too bad. We have to have a garage.

Questions

1 Does the realtor have a house for sale?
2 Is it in a quiet neighborhood?
3 How many sons and daughters do Mr. and Mrs. Nolan have?
4 Do they have to buy a big house?
5 How many bedrooms does the house have?
6 What does it also have?
7 Does it have a garage?
8 Do Mr. and Mrs. Nolan have to have a garage?

Personal Questions

1 Do you have a house?
2 Is the house big or small?
3 Where is the house?
4 Does it have a garage?

5 How many rooms does it have?
6 What is upstairs?
7 What is downstairs?
8 Is the house new or old?

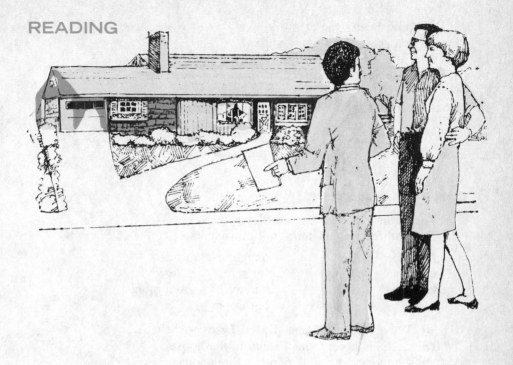

Mr. and Mrs. Davis are teachers. They live in a small house in the city. They have two sons and two daughters.

The Davis family has to buy a new house. Every morning Mrs. Davis reads the newspapers. Today she finds a house for sale. It has a living room, kitchen, bathroom, three bedrooms, and a garage.

Mr. and Mrs. Davis go to see the house. The house doesn't have a big yard, but it's near a park. It's also near a school and many stores. Mr. and Mrs. Davis are happy with the house. What about the price? Is the house very expensive? No, it's not expensive. Mr. and Mrs. Davis buy the house. Now the Davis family has a new house.

Questions

1 Are Mr. and Mrs. Davis teachers?
2 Where do they live?
3 Do they have a big house?
4 How many sons and daughters do they have?
5 Does the Davis family have to buy a new house?
6 Does Mrs. Davis read the newspapers every morning?
7 Does she find a house for sale today?
8 Does it have a living room and a kitchen?
9 How many bedrooms does it have?
10 Does it have a garage?
11 Do Mr. and Mrs. Davis go to see the house?
12 Does the house have a big yard?

13 Is the house near a park?
14 Is it near a school and many stores?
15 Are Mr. and Mrs. Davis happy with the house?
16 Is the house very expensive?
17 Do Mr. and Mrs. Davis buy the house?
18 Does the Davis family have a new house now?

LESSON REVIEW

I Complete the sentences.

The bathroom is ____, not downstairs. →
The bathroom is upstairs, not downstairs.

father	finds	daughters	near
mother	family	for sale	new
keys	price	has to	morning
rooms	expensive	bathroom	

1 Mr. Davis is the father and Mrs. Davis is the ____.
2 The ____ is a very small room in the house.
3 Mr. Connors is a ____. He has three sons.
4 What is the ____ of the house? Is it expensive?
5 How many ____ does the house have?
6 I have to buy a house. Do you have a house ____?
7 They don't buy the car. It's very ____.
8 The house is not old. It's ____.
9 She reads the newspaper every ____.
10 The house is ____ many stores.
11 Mrs. Davis has two ____, Marie and Helen.
12 Mr. Gordon ____ go to the doctor today.
13 Where are the ____? I have to drive the car.
14 She ____ a newspaper near the door every morning.
15 Mr. and Mrs. Ross have a big ____. They have three sons and two daughters.

II Answer the questions. Write a story.

Do you have a big family?
How many sons and daughters do you have?
Do you have to buy a new house?
Do you see a house for sale in the newspaper?
How many rooms does the house have?
Is the living room downstairs or upstairs?
What is upstairs?
Is the house very expensive?
Do you have to call the realtor?

LESSON 4

NEW WORDS

1   The bank is large.
    The tellers work in the bank.
    There are many customers in
        line.
    The tellers help the customers.
    They speak to the customers.
    The customers thank the
        tellers.

2 The woman deposits money.
 She makes a deposit.
 The teller takes the money
   from the woman.
 He takes the passbook and the
   deposit slip too.
 He puts the money in the
   drawer.

3 The man withdraws money.
 He makes a withdrawal.
 He gives the teller a withdrawal
   slip.
 The man doesn't want a check.
 He gets cash.

4 The teller looks up again.
   There is a woman in line.
   The teller asks, "Do you need
     help?"
   The woman says, "Yes, I do."
   The woman needs a new
     passbook.

SAVINGS →

A Answer the questions.

1   Is the bank large?
2   Do the tellers work in the bank?
3   Are there many customers in line?
4   Do the tellers help the customers?
5   Do they speak to the customers?
6   Do the customers thank the tellers?
7   Who deposits money?
8   Does she make a deposit?
9   What does the teller take from the woman?
10 Does he take the passbook and the deposit slip too?
11 Where does he put the money?
12 Does the man withdraw money?
13 Does he make a withdrawal?
14 What does he give the teller?
15 Does the man want a check?
16 What does he get?
17 Does the teller look up again?
18 Is there a woman in line?
19 What does the teller ask?
20 What does the woman need?

B Complete the sentences.

1   She is a teller. She works in a ＿＿＿ in the city.
2   The woman puts money in the bank. She makes a ＿＿＿.

3   The man gets money from the teller. He makes a _____.
4   A _____ works in a bank and helps customers.
5   The teller always puts the money in a _____.
6   He does not want cash; he wants a _____.
7   There are always many _____ in line in the bank.
8   The teller _____ up and sees a customer in line.

MORE NEW WORDS

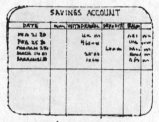

savings account

checking account

STRUCTURE

Verbs like *to help*

He helps, she helps

A   Repeat.
Miss Day thanks the teller.
Mr. Troy looks up.
A teller helps many customers.

B   Answer.
Does he work in a bank?
Does he help customers?
Does the teller always look up?
Does the man make a withdrawal?
Does the woman want cash?
Does she always get cash?
Does the customer speak to the teller?
Does the girl thank the woman?
Does she take the money?
Does she put the money in the drawer?
Does she always deposit money?

I help, you help, we help, they help

A   Repeat.
I always thank the teller.
You speak English every day.
We want cash.
They take the passbook.

B   Answer. Use *I*.

Do you always thank the teller?
Do you want to make a deposit?
Do you help many customers?
Do you put the money in the drawer?
Do you speak English?

C   Answer. Use *we*.

Do you work in a hospital?
Do you help the doctors?
Do you want cash or a check?
Do you get cash from the teller?
Do you take the passbook from the teller?

D   Answer.

Do the customers speak to the tellers?
Do they make deposits?
Do they speak to the banker too?
Do they want a checking account?
Do they thank the tellers?

E   Follow the model.

Who works in a bank? →
You work in a bank.

Who wants a checking account?
Who speaks to the teller?
Who puts money in the checking account?
Who makes a withdrawal?
Who thanks the teller?

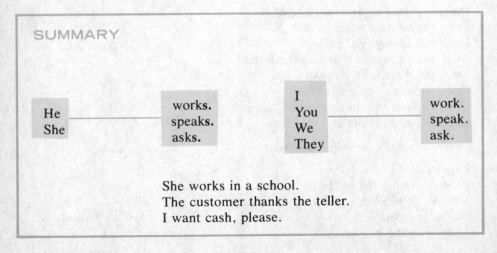

SUMMARY

| He She | — | works. speaks. asks. | I You We They | — | work. speak. ask. |

She works in a school.
The customer thanks the teller.
I want cash, please.

In the bank

Choose the correct word.

> A teller (work, works) in a bank. →
> A teller works in a bank.

1 The man and I (take, takes) the money.
2 You (make, makes) a deposit every day.
3 Tellers (help, helps) customers.
4 You and I (ask, asks) the banker.
5 I (speak, speaks) to the doctor.
6 The student (want, wants) the book.
7 A nurse (work, works) in a hospital.
8 We (thank, thanks) the teacher.
9 They (deposit, deposits) money every day.
10 I (put, puts) the chairs in the room.

Short answers with auxiliary *do*

Doesn't

A Repeat.
Does Mr. Ross work in a bank? No, he doesn't.
Does Mrs. Lee speak English? No, she doesn't.
Does the house have a big yard? No, it doesn't.

59

B **Answer. Use _no_ and a short answer.**
Does Mr. Carr live in the country?
Does he drive to the bank?
Does he have a car?
Does Mrs. Jones study every day?
Does she need help?
Does she buy many magazines?
Does the house have a big kitchen?
Does it have three bedrooms?
Does it have a dining room?

Don't

A **Repeat.**
Do Mr. and Mrs. Ross swim every day? No, they don't.
Do you have a deposit slip? No, I don't.
Do you and Mr. Carr have to go to the bank? No, we don't.
Do I get a passbook here? No, you don't.

B **Answer. Use _no_ and a short answer.**
Do the tellers work every day?
Do they live near the bank?
Do Mr. and Mrs. Lee have a house?
Do you work in a bank?
Do you go to the bank every day?
Do you drive a big car?
Do you and Mrs. Kane go to school every day?
Do you study every day?
Do you read many magazines?
Do I have to study English?
Do I need a new car?
Do I make a deposit here?

Does

A **Repeat.**
Does Mr. Miller want cash? Yes, he does.
Does Mrs. Lee have a car? Yes, she does.
Does the store have many customers? Yes, it does.

B **Answer. Use _yes_ and a short answer.**
Does Miss Baker go to school?
Does she study English?
Does she drive every day?
Does Mr. Allen go to the store every day?
Does he buy newspapers?
Does he want a house in the country?
Does the store have magazines?
Does it have newspapers?
Does it have pictures?

The man makes a deposit

NEXT TELLER PLEASE

Do

A Repeat.

Do Mr. and Mrs. Lee help the boy? Yes, they do.
Do you need money? Yes, I do.
Do you and Mrs. Stone have a savings account? Yes, we do.
Do I need a deposit slip? Yes, you do.

B Answer. Use *yes* and a short answer.

Do Mr. and Mrs. Warren live in the country?
Do they swim every day?
Do they drive to the city?
Do you go to school in the city?
Do you live near the school?
Do you study English?
Do you and Miss Day go to the country?
Do you take a picnic basket?
Do you swim in the lake?
Do I buy many newspapers?
Do I need a checking account?
Do I make a deposit here?

SUMMARY

Does	he / she / it	have a garage?	**No,**	he / she / it	**doesn't.**
Do	you / I / we / they	drive every day?	**No,**	I (we) / you / you (we) / they	**don't.**
Does	he / she / it	leave in the morning?	**Yes,**	he / she / it	**does.**
Do	you / I / we / they	need help?	**Yes,**	I (we) / you / we (you) / they	**do.**

Do you have a small car? Yes, I do.
Does Mrs. Lee speak English? No, she doesn't.

Writing Practice

Write the correct short answers. Follow the models.

> Do the tellers help the customers? *Yes* →
> Yes, they do.
>
> Does the house have a garage? *No* →
> No, it doesn't.

1   Does Mr. Lee work in the city? *No*
2   Does the magazine have pictures? *Yes*
3   Do you speak to the teacher every day? *Yes*
4   Do the customers thank the tellers? *Yes*
5   Do you have to leave now? *No*
6   Do I speak English in school? *Yes*
7   Does Miss Taylor always hurry to school? *No*
8   Do you and Mr. Clark live in the country? *No*
9   Does Mr. Weaver work in the hospital? *Yes*
10 Do the teachers drive to school? *No*
11 Do I need a deposit slip? *No*
12 Does Miss Simmons buy a newspaper every day? *Yes*
13 Does the hospital have a garage? *No*
14 Do you and Mrs. Troy have to buy a new car? *Yes*

There is, there are

A   Repeat.

Is there a check in the drawer?
Yes, there is a check in the drawer.
Yes, there's a check in the drawer.

Are there many tellers in the bank?
Yes, there are many tellers in the bank.

How many customers are there in line?
There are ten customers in line.

B   Answer.

Is there a hospital in the city?
Is there a telephone in the kitchen?
Is there a house near the lake?
Is there a car in the garage?
Is there a chair in the yard?

Are there many customers in the bank?
Are there many cars for sale?
Are there four chairs in the kitchen?
Are there two bedrooms upstairs?
Are there many stores near the house?

How many boys are there in the family?
How many rooms are there in the house?
How many doctors are there in the hospital?
How many tellers are there in the bank?

Short answers with *there is, there are*

A   Repeat.

Is there a check in the drawer? Yes, there is.
Are there many cars in the park? Yes, there are.

B   Answer.

Is there a school in the neighborhood?
Is there a daughter in the family?
Is there a key in the door?
Is there a store near the house?

Are there many hospitals in the city?
Are there two tellers in the bank?
Are there many customers in line?
Are there many lakes in the country?

SUMMARY

Is there a telephone in the room?
Yes, **there is.**
There is a telephone in the room.

Are there two chairs in the kitchen?
Yes, **there are.**
There are two chairs in the kitchen.

There is a table in the living room.
There are newspapers for sale in the store.

Writing Practice

Complete the sentences. Use *There's, There are, Is there,* or *Are there.*

_____ three bedrooms upstairs. →
There are three bedrooms upstairs.

1 _____ a withdrawal slip in the drawer.
2 _____ pictures in the magazine.
3 _____ a bathroom downstairs?
4 _____ many customers in the store?
5 _____ a telephone in the living room.
6 _____ a house for sale?
7 _____ two cars near the school.
8 _____ a nurse in the room.
9 _____ always many tellers in the bank.
10 _____ a big kitchen downstairs.

CONVERSATION

In the bank

Customer	Are you a teller here?
Mrs. Hart	Yes, I am. Do you need help?
Customer	Yes, I do. I want to make a withdrawal. Here is the withdrawal slip.
Mrs. Hart	Do you have a passbook?
Customer	Yes. Here it is.
Mrs. Hart	Do you want cash or a check?
Customer	Cash, please.
Mrs. Hart	Here is the money and the passbook.
Customer	Thank you very much.

Questions

1 Is Mrs. Hart a teller?
2 Does the customer need help?
3 What does the customer want?
4 Does the customer have a passbook?
5 Does the customer want cash or a check?
6 Does Mrs. Hart give the customer the money and the passbook?
7 Does the customer thank Mrs. Hart?

Personal Questions

1 Do you go to the bank sometimes?
2 Do you sometimes make a withdrawal or a deposit?
3 Do you always need a withdrawal slip or a deposit slip?
4 Do you need a passbook too?
5 Do you always want cash when you make a withdrawal?
6 Do you always thank the teller?

READING

The bank teller

Mr. Irwin is a teller. He works in a large bank in the city. Every day he speaks to many customers.

There are many customers in the bank today. Mr. Irwin looks up and sees a man in line. The man wants to make a deposit. Mr. Irwin helps the man. He takes the money and the passbook from the man. He puts the money in a drawer and makes the deposit. The customer thanks Mr. Irwin and leaves.

Mr. Irwin looks up again. Now there is a woman in line.

"Do I get a new passbook here?"

"Yes, you do," says Mr. Irwin. He gives the woman a new passbook.

Mr. Irwin looks up again. There are many customers in line. Mr. Irwin helps many customers every day.

Questions

1   Is Mr. Irwin a teller?
2   Where does he work?
3   Does he speak to many customers every day?
4   Are there many customers in the bank today?
5   Does Mr. Irwin look up and see a man in line?
6   What does the man want?
7   Does Mr. Irwin help the man?
8   Who takes the money and the passbook from the man?
9   Where does he put the money?
10   Does he make the deposit?
11   Does the customer thank Mr. Irwin?
12   Is there a woman in line now?
13   Does she want a new passbook?
14   Does Mr. Irwin help the woman?
15   Does Mr. Irwin look up again?
16   Are there many customers in line?
17   Does Mr. Irwin help many customers every day?

LESSON REVIEW

I Complete the sentences.

The teller puts the money in the _____. →
The teller puts the money in the drawer.

help	look	bank	want
make	thanks	work	takes
puts	asks	cash	from
deposit	line	withdrawal	savings

  1   Mr. White is a teller in a large _____.
2–3 She makes a small _____ in a _____ account.
  4   I _____ Mr. Trent find the house.
  5   They are bankers. They _____ in a bank.
  6   I _____ up and see many customers in line.
  7   The man _____ the teller and leaves the bank.
  8   I _____ to make a deposit.
  9   He needs money. He goes to the bank and makes a _____.
10 Do you want _____ or a check?
11 The teller _____ the money from the drawer.
12 There are many customers in _____ in the bank today.
13 Does he _____ a deposit every day?
14 The woman _____ the man, "Are you a new teller here?"
15 Mrs. Peters _____ the checks in the drawer.
16 We take the passbook _____ the teller and leave the bank.

II Answer the questions. Write a story.

Do tellers work in a bank?
Do they help many customers every day?
Does a man in line want to make a deposit?
Does the teller take the money and the passbook from the man?
Does he (she) put the money in a drawer?
Does he (she) make the deposit?
Does a woman want to make a withdrawal?
Does she give the teller a withdrawal slip?
Does she want cash or a check?
Does the teller take the money from the drawer?
Does he (she) give the money to the customer?
Do the customers thank the tellers and leave?

LESSON 5

NEW WORDS

1 The bus stop is on the corner.
  Miss Lyons waits for the bus
      every day.
  She takes the bus to work.
  It is cold and gray today.
  Miss Lyons has an umbrella.
  She is alone.
  Here comes a bus.

2 The bus runs often.
   It runs every ten minutes.
   Mr. Cole meets a friend at the
      bus stop.

3 The bus stops.
   A man gets off the bus.
   A woman gets on.
   She pays the fare.
   It is rush hour.
   The bus is crowded, but it isn't
      full.
   There is an empty seat in the
      back.

4   It is a busy morning in the
      center of the city.
    There are many people outside.
    The stores aren't open.
    Miss Ames walks across the
      street.
    The office is open.
    The office is in an office
      building.

5   Mr. Lee wakes up at eight
      o'clock.
    He looks at the clock.
    Mrs. Lee is ready to leave.

A   Answer the questions.

    1   Where is the bus stop?
    2   Who waits for the bus every day?
    3   What does she take to work?
    4   Is it cold and gray today?
    5   What does Miss Lyons have?

6   Is she alone?
7   Does the bus run often?
8   How often does the bus run?
9   Who does Mr. Cole meet?
10 Does the bus stop?
11 Does a man get off the bus?
12 Who gets on?
13 What does she pay?
14 Is the bus crowded?
15 Is there an empty seat?
16 Is it a busy morning in the center of the city?
17 Are there many people outside?
18 Who walks across the street?
19 Is the office open?
20 Where is the office?
21 Who wakes up at eight o'clock?
22 What time does he wake up?
23 Does he look at the clock?
24 Is Mrs. Lee ready to leave?

B Complete the sentences.

1   People wait for a bus at a _____.
2   The bus stop is on the _____.
3   When you get on the bus, you have to pay the _____.
4   Many people _____ the bus to work.
5   They walk across the _____ and go to the office.

STRUCTURE

Noun plurals: *book/books*

A Repeat.
The checks are in the drawer.
The teacher helps the students.
I need two deposit slips.

B Answer.
Are the banks crowded today?
Are the books on the table?
Are the lakes very large?
Are the clocks upstairs?
Are the parks near the house?
Are the streets crowded?
Are the students in school?
Are the seats empty?
Are the baskets in the kitchen?
Are the deposit slips in the drawer?
Are the bus stops near the office?

SUMMARY

key	book	seat	deposit slip
keys	books	seats	deposit slips

The books are in the bedroom.
The keys are in the car.

Writing Practice

Make the words plural. Follow the model.

(student)   The _____ are ready. →
The students are ready.

1   (check)   Do you need two _____?
2   (bank)   There are two _____ on the corner.
3   (slip)   The teller has the withdrawal _____.
4   (street)   There are many cars in the _____.
5   (minute)   The bus runs every ten _____.
6   (park)   The city has five _____.
7   (passbook)   The _____ are in the drawer.
8   (bus stop)   There are two _____ near the house.

Contractions *isn't* and *aren't*

Isn't

A Repeat.
The car is not in the garage.
The car isn't in the garage.

Mrs. Baker is not here.
Mrs. Baker isn't here.

B Practice. Change *is not* to *isn't*.
The check is not in the drawer.
The store is not open today.
The teacher is not in school.
She is not downstairs.
The teller is not busy today.
Mr. Allen is not on the bus.
The banker is not ready.
The school is not in the city.

A crowded city street

C Answer. Use *isn't*.

>Is the doctor in the office? →
>No, the doctor isn't in the office.

Is the umbrella in the bedroom?
Is the car expensive?
Is the bank open today?
Is Miss Lyons in the office?
Is Mrs. Miller a nurse?
Is the hospital old?
Is Mr. Lee in the hospital?
Is the house for sale?

Aren't

A Repeat.
The boys are not in the park.
The boys aren't in the park.

We are not teachers.
We aren't teachers.

You are not busy today.
You aren't busy today.

B Practice. Change *are not* to *aren't*.
The keys are not in the car.
The bedrooms are not downstairs.
The customers are not in line.
We are not ready.
You are not happy today.
The students are not quiet today.
Mr. Lee and I are not always here.
The stores are not crowded today.

C Answer. Use *aren't*.

>Are the books on the table? →
>No, the books aren't on the table.

Are the stores open today?
Are the streets crowded?
Are the tellers ready to leave?
Are the parks large?
Are you and Miss King busy today?
Are you teachers?
Am I American?
Am I a student?

Where is the

Taking the bus

SUMMARY

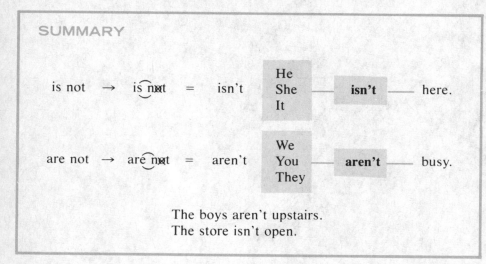

is not → is n~o~t = isn't

| He She It | — **isn't** — here. |

are not → are n~o~t = aren't

| We You They | — **aren't** — busy. |

The boys aren't upstairs.
The store isn't open.

Writing Practice

Complete the sentences. Use *isn't* or *aren't*.

1 The boys _____ in school.
2 The lawyers _____ in the office today.
3 You _____ a banker.
4 The school _____ old.
5 Miss Lyons _____ in the hospital.
6 We _____ in line.
7 The banks _____ open today.
8 The stores _____ crowded today.
9 The fare _____ expensive.
10 We _____ at the bus stop.

Article *an*

A Repeat.

Do you have an umbrella?
Mr. Ross is an English teacher.
Miss Lyons works in an office.

B Answer.

Do they have an old house?
Do they have an expensive car?
Does the doctor have an office here?
Do you see an open door?
Do you work in an office building?
Do you have an empty basket?
Do you have an American friend?
Does Mr. Lee have an English book?
Does he work in an office building?

SUMMARY

an American book	**a** large office
an empty drawer	**a** check
an injection	**a** drawer
an office	**a** seat
an umbrella	**a** deposit

Is it an expensive car?
You need an umbrella.

Writing Practice

Complete the sentences. Use *a* or *an*.

1 Mrs. Jones has ＿＿＿ American car.
2 The lawyer has ＿＿＿ office in the city.
3 Do you see ＿＿＿ empty seat?
4 We don't want ＿＿＿ expensive house.
5 The customer needs ＿＿＿ new passbook.
6 Do you want ＿＿＿ upstairs room?
7 Miss Lyons has ＿＿＿ English magazine.
8 Is there ＿＿＿ doctor in the building?

CONVERSATION

Where is the bus stop?

Mr. Lang   Excuse me. Where is the bus stop?
Miss Evers   For the bus to the city?
Mr. Lang   Yes.
Miss Evers   There it is, on the corner.
Mr. Lang   Does the bus run often?
Miss Evers   It runs every thirty minutes when it isn't rush hour. Here comes a bus now.
Mr. Lang   I have to hurry then. Thank you.
Miss Evers   Good-bye.

Questions

1   Where is the bus stop?
2   Who is going to the city?
3   Does he want the bus to the city?
4   How often does the bus run?
5   Does Miss Evers see a bus?
6   Does Mr. Lang have to hurry?
7   Does he thank Miss Evers?

Personal Questions

1   Do you take a bus to work?
2   Where is the bus stop?
3   Do you wait on the corner?
4   Are there always many people at the bus stop?
5   Does the bus run often?
6   How often does the bus run?
7   Do you pay the fare when you get on?
8   Is the bus always crowded?

READING

Taking the bus

It is a cold gray morning in a large city. Miss Carter wakes up and looks at the clock. It's eight o'clock. She has to hurry.

In thirty minutes Miss Carter is ready to leave. She takes an umbrella and goes outside. She walks to the bus stop on the corner. Sometimes she meets an old friend, Mrs. Laker, at the bus stop. Mrs. Laker isn't there today, and Miss Carter waits for the bus alone. The bus comes in five minutes. Miss Carter gets on and pays the fare. It's rush hour. The bus is crowded, but it isn't full. Miss Carter finds an empty seat in the back.

The bus stops in the center of the city. Miss Carter gets off. She walks across the street to the office. It's a busy morning. The streets of the city are crowded. The stores aren't open, but the office buildings are full of people. It's nine o'clock.

Questions

1 Is it a cold gray morning?
2 Who wakes up?
3 Does she look at the clock?
4 What time is it?
5 Does she have to hurry?
6 Is she ready to leave in thirty minutes?
7 What does she take?
8 Does she go outside?
9 Who does she meet at the bus stop sometimes?
10 Is Mrs. Laker there today?

11   Who waits for the bus alone?
12   Does the bus come in five minutes?
13   What does Miss Carter pay?
14   Is the bus crowded?
15   Is it full?
16   Where does Miss Carter find an empty seat?
17   Where does the bus stop?
18   Does Miss Carter walk across the street to the office?
19   Are the streets crowded?
20   Are the stores open?
21   Are the office buildings full of people?

LESSON REVIEW

I   Complete the sentences.

streets	isn't	bus	o'clock	gets on
seats	every	aren't	office	meets
alone	an	a	corner	crowded

1   Mr. Williams wakes up at seven _____ every morning.
2   The banks _____ open today.
3   The lawyer has an _____ in the city.
4   There are two empty _____ on the bus.
5   Sometimes Miss Lyons _____ a friend on the bus.
6   The stores are very _____ today.
7   Mr. Simmons isn't with a friend. He's _____.
8   The bus stop is on the _____.
9   Do you have _____ umbrella?
10 Mrs. Gray _____ the bus and pays the fare.
11 The teacher _____ in school today.
12 Is there _____ store in the building?
13 It's rush hour. The _____ of the city are full of cars.
14 The bus to the city runs _____ fifteen minutes.
15 I take a _____ to work every day.

II   Answer the questions. Write a story.

Is it a gray morning?
Are there many people at the bus stop?
Do they have umbrellas?
When the bus comes, do they get on and pay the fare?
Is it rush hour?
Is the bus crowded?
Do the people get off when the bus stops in the city?
Do they walk across the street to the office?
Is it a busy morning?
Are the streets of the city full of people?

LESSON 6

NEW WORDS

1 It's early.
   The Lang family always gets up
      early.
   Mary eats breakfast.
   Mrs. Lang just has coffee.
   Tom washes.
   Mr. Lang dresses.

2 It's late.
   The woman rushes to the
      subway station.
   She has to catch the train.

3 The man changes trains.
   He gets off the first train.
   He crosses the platform.
   He gets on another train.

4 The ride on the subway is not
     long.
  The subway is crowded, but
     fast.
  Cars wait in traffic, subways
     don't.

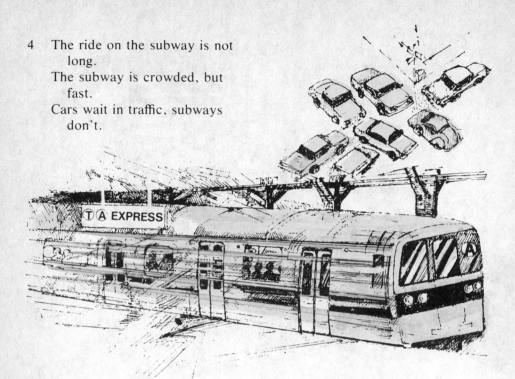

A Answer the questions.

1 Do Mr. and Mrs. Lang always get up early?
2 Who eats breakfast?
3 What does Mrs. Lang have?
4 Who washes?
5 Who dresses?
6 Is it late?
7 Does the woman rush to the subway station?
8 Does she have to catch the train?
9 Does the man change trains?
10 Does he get off the first train?
11 Does he cross the platform?
12 Does he get on another train?
13 Is the ride on the subway long?
14 Is the subway fast?
15 Do cars wait in traffic?
16 Do subways wait in traffic?

B Complete the sentences.

1 I _____ early every morning.
2 They don't take the bus; they always take the _____.
3 She has to walk across the _____ and change trains.
4 Do you always _____ the first train?

5   I am _____; I have to rush.
6   Every morning he washes, dresses, and eats _____.
7   The woman walks downstairs to the subway _____.
8   During rush hour cars always have to wait in _____.

MORE NEW WORDS

to close   to push

STRUCTURE

Verbs like *to wash*

She washes, he washes

A   Repeat.
Mr. Lang washes the car often.
The woman closes the door.
She crosses the street.

B   Substitute.

```
      dresses
She   washes   every morning.
      rushes
```

```
      closes the door.
He    catches the train.
      changes trains often.
```

C   Answer.
Does Mrs. Lang dress for work?
Does she dress in the bedroom?
Does she close the door?
Does Mr. Gordon rush to the station?
Does he catch the train?
Does he change trains?
Does the girl cross the platform?
Does she push the man?
Does the door close?
Does the boy wash the car?

I wash, you wash, we wash, they wash

A Repeat.
I change trains here.
You always catch the first train.
We dress for work.
The boys wash very fast.

B Answer.
Do you rush across the street?
Do you change trains at Center Street?
Do I catch the train here?
Do I cross the platform?
Do you and Miss Dale dress for school?
Do you and Mr. Post rush every morning?
Do doctors always rush to work?
Do they dress fast?

At the subway station

SUMMARY

| She / He | — reads. | She / He | — works. | She / He | — dresses. |

She / He — reads.

She / He — works.

She / He — dresses.

I / You / We / They — read.

I / You / We / They — work.

I / You / We / They — dress.

She buys a newspaper every day.
The customer wants a check.
He always catches the early train.

Follow the model.

>The man (close) the door. →
>The man closes the door.

1 Sometimes the girl (wash) the car.
2 She (cross) the street and goes to work.
3 We get up early and (dress) for school.
4 You are late; you (rush) to the office.
5 The man (push) the car across the street.
6 I (change) trains at Lexington Avenue.
7 Do they always (catch) the first bus?
8 He gets up, (wash), and eats breakfast.
9 Do you always (rush) in the morning?
10 The door (close) and the train leaves.

Imperative form of verbs

Affirmative imperative

A **Repeat.**
Please close the door, Mr. Lee.
Miss Lyons, come here, please.
Girls, call the doctor now.

B **Practice.**
Tell a student to wash the car.
Tell a student to read the books.
Tell a student to buy a newspaper.
Tell a student to take an umbrella.
Tell a student to find the keys.
Tell two students to go downstairs.
Tell two students to help the teacher.
Tell two students to look at the picture.
Tell two students to carry the basket.
Tell two students to cross the street.

Negative imperative

A **Repeat.**
Don't go to the bank, Mrs. Gray.
Don't close the door, boys.
Please don't push.

B **Practice.**
Tell a student not to get up.
Tell a student not to wait.

Tell a student not to take the subway.
Tell a student not to cross the street.
Tell a student not to say no.
Tell two students not to walk fast.
Tell two students not to rush.
Tell two students not to leave the building.
Tell two students not to go to the store today.
Tell two students not to get off here.

SUMMARY

Take the subway to Bond Street.
Girls, **get up** now.
Please **close** the door, Mrs. Lang.

Don't take the bus.
Please **don't drive** fast.
Don't rush—it's early.

Cars wait in traffic.

The subway is fast.

Writing Practice

A Follow the models.

> Do I have to go upstairs? →
> Yes, go upstairs!
>
> Do we have to eat breakfast? →
> Yes, eat breakfast!

1 Do I have to dress fast?
2 Do I have to take the bus to the city?
3 Do I have to cross the platform?
4 Do we have to wash the car?
5 Do we have to go to the hospital?
6 Do we have to leave the building?

B Follow the models.

> We want to wait for the teacher. →
> No, don't wait for the teacher.
>
> I want to read the newspaper now. →
> No, don't read the newspaper now.

1 We want to swim in the lake.
2 We want to help the boy.
3 We want to walk in the park.
4 I want to go to the store.
5 I want to wash the car now.
6 I want to buy the big car.

Preposition *at*

A Repeat.
There are many people at the bus stop.
The train stops at Market Street.
There are two customers at the table.

B   Answer.
Does the bus stop at the bank?
Is the subway crowded at rush hour?
Do you call Miss Hill at the office?
Are you busy at work?
Does Mr. Marlow meet a friend at the subway station?
Do they change trains at First Avenue?
Does the Ross family eat at the lake sometimes?
Do you read the newspaper at the table?
Do many people get off at Bank Street?
Do they have to wait at the bus stop?

SUMMARY

at the bus stop   **at** the table

Miss Lyons waits for Miss Hunter at the bus stop.
They get off the bus at Center Street.

Writing Practice

Answer the questions. Use *at*.

    (bank)   Where is Mr. Harrow? →
    Mr. Harrow is at the bank.

1   (Main Street)   Where do you change trains?
2   (corner)   Where does the bus stop?
3   (subway station)   Where is Mr. Ross?
4   (office)   Where is Miss Lyons?
5   (bus stop)   Where do the friends meet?
6   (work)   Where do you read the newspaper?
7   (Hill Street)   Where do you get off the bus?
8   (rush hour)   When is the bus stop crowded?

CONVERSATION

At the subway station

Mrs. Allen	Excuse me. How do I get to Lexington Street?
Mr. Banks	Lexington Street. Hmm. OK. Take the train to Second Avenue. Then get off and change for the train to Grover Square.
Mrs. Allen	Do I have to go upstairs at Second Avenue?
Mr. Banks	No. Just cross the platform when you get off.
Mrs. Allen	Is Lexington Street near Grover Square?
Mr. Banks	Yes. When you go upstairs, cross the square. It's the street with the large stores.
Mrs. Allen	OK. Thanks very much.

Questions

1 Who wants to go to Lexington Street?
2 Where does she change trains?
3 Does she have to go upstairs at Second Avenue?
4 Is Lexington Street near Grover Square?
5 Does Lexington Street have large stores?
6 Does Mrs. Allen thank Mr. Banks?

Personal Questions

1 Do you take the train to work?
2 Where do you get off?
3 Do you have to change trains?
4 Do you cross the platform?
5 Is the ride on the train very long?
6 Do you leave early every morning?

The subway is fast

Mrs. Lang lives in a big city. She gets up early every morning. She washes, dresses, and eats breakfast. Then she leaves for work. Mrs. Lang doesn't drive to work. She takes the subway every day.

Today Mrs. Lang is late. She rushes to the subway station. She walks downstairs and catches the train. She takes the first train to Bank Street. There she gets off.

Mrs. Lang has to change trains at Bank Street. She crosses the platform and waits for another train.

At rush hour the subway is very crowded, but it is very fast. Cars have to wait in rush hour traffic. Subways don't.

Questions

1   Does Mrs. Lang get up early every morning?
2   Does she wash and dress?
3   Does she eat breakfast?
4   Does she drive to work?
5   Does she take the subway every day?
6   Is Mrs. Lang late today?
7   Does she rush to the subway station?
8   Does she catch the first train to Bank Street?
9   Where does she get off?

10   Does she have to change trains?
11   Does she cross the platform?
12   Is the subway very fast?
13   Do subways wait in rush hour traffic?

LESSON REVIEW

I   Complete the sentences.

We have to hurry to the subway _____. →
We have to hurry to the subway station.

early	dresses	catch
breakfast	fast	platform
rush	ride	another
closes	long	change
at	get up	

1   I eat a big _____ in the morning.
2   It's not _____. It's very late.
3   The woman _____ in the bedroom.
4   The bank always _____ early.
5   They're late. They have to _____ to the bus stop.
6   Mr. Lang crosses the _____ and gets on another train.
7   Does she _____ the first train to Wall Street every day?
8   Subways are very _____; they don't have to wait in traffic.
9   Is it a long _____ on the train?
10   We have to go upstairs and catch _____ train.
11   Do you have to _____ early every morning?
12   Mr. Hill changes trains _____ Main Street.
13   Does it take _____ to drive to the city?
14   You have to get off here and _____ trains.

II   Answer the questions. Write a story.

Do you get up early in the morning?
Do you wash, dress, and eat breakfast?
Do you take the subway to work?
Do you rush to the subway station?
Do you catch the early train?
Do you change trains sometimes?
Do you get off and cross the platform?
Do you catch another train?
Is the subway very fast?
Are you always at work very early?

LESSON 7

NEW WORDS

1   A new day is just beginning in
        the post office.
    The clerk is at the window.
    She is beginning to work.
    The letter carrier is going out.
    He has to deliver the mail.
    He is wearing a hat and coat.

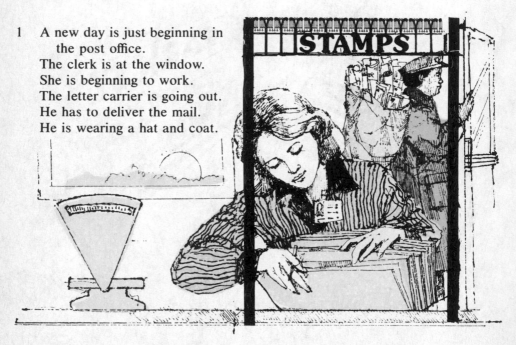

2 The woman is writing a letter.
   The name and address are on
      the envelope.
   The package has just one
      airmail stamp.

3 Many people are standing in
      line.
   Some are buying stamps.
   Others are mailing letters.
   The clerk sends the man to the
      next window.

STAMPS

4   The woman is putting a letter
        in the mailbox.
    The man is still putting the mail
        on the truck.
    The truck is leaving soon.
    The girl is running.

each   every
        You have to put a stamp on each letter.

A   Answer the questions.

1   Is a new day just beginning?
2   Where is the clerk?
3   Is she beginning to work?
4   Who is going out?
5   What does he have to deliver?
6   What is he wearing?
7   Is the woman writing a letter?
8   What is she doing?
9   Are the name and address on the envelope?
10 Does the package have just one airmail stamp?
11 Are many people standing in line?
12 Are some buying stamps?
13 What are they doing?
14 Are others mailing letters?
15 What are they doing?
16 Does the clerk send the man to the next window?
17 Where does the woman put the letter?
18 Is the man still putting the mail on the truck?
19 Is the truck leaving soon?
20 Is the girl walking or running?

B True or false. Correct each false statement.

1 A lawyer delivers the mail.
2 A teller works in a post office.
3 We put letters in a mailbox.
4 Each envelope needs a name and address.
5 You buy stamps at the bank.
6 A clerk works at a window in the post office.

MORE NEW WORDS

jacket

shirt

suit

pants

dress

shoes

blouse

skirt

sweater

Present progressive tense

He, she, it

A   Repeat.
Mrs. Ross is working now.
She's working now.

Mr. Caine is eating breakfast.
He's eating breakfast.

The truck is pushing the car.
It's pushing the car.

B   Answer.
Is the boy crossing the street?
Is he going to the store?
Is he hurrying?
Is he wearing a jacket?

Is Miss Baker working now?
Is she helping the customers?
Is she speaking to Mr. Lee?
Is she looking at the clock?

Is the bus going to the city?
Is it waiting at the bus stop?

I

A   Repeat.
I'm mailing two letters.
I'm going to the post office.

B   Answer.
Are you wearing new shoes?
Are you reading a new book?
Are you waiting for the clerk?
Are you studying now?
Are you going out?
Are you sending a package
    to Miss Lee?

What is the letter carrier wearing?

You, we, they

A   Repeat.
You're studying English.
Are you studying now?

We're buying a house.

Mr. and Mrs. Ross are going to the lake.
They're going to the lake.

B   Answer.
Are you and Miss Clark helping the boys?
Are you eating now?
Are you sending the package airmail?
Are you mailing many letters?
Are you waiting for the teacher?

Are the tellers working late today?
Are the students speaking to the teacher?
Are the doctors rushing to the hospital?
Are they crossing the street now?
Are they wearing suits?

C   Ask.
Ask a student if he is calling a lawyer.
Ask a student if she is wearing a new dress.
Ask a student if he is wearing a new sweater.
Ask a student if she is reading the newspaper.
Ask two students if they are standing in line.
Ask two students if they are going to the post office.

D   Follow the model.

She calls the doctor every day. →
She's calling the doctor now.

He wears a jacket every day.
They wash the car every day.
I go to work every day.
We eat breakfast every day.
She studies every day.
They deliver the mail every day.

speak	speak + ing	=	**speaking**
pay	pay + ing	=	**paying**
rush	rush + ing	=	**rushing**
ask	ask + ing	=	**asking**

I am (I'm)
She is (She's)
He is (He's)
It is (It's) —————— going now.
You are (You're)
We are (We're)
They are (They're)

I'm buying a new suit.
Miss Lyons is speaking to the teller.
They're waiting for a bus.

Writing Practice

A Rewrite the sentences. Use contractions.

1 We are buying airmail stamps.
2 She is standing in line.
3 It is going to the city.
4 They are hurrying to the bus stop.
5 I am working fast.
6 He is delivering the letters.
7 You are walking fast.

B Answer the questions. Use the cues.

Where is Miss Lyons going? *to the post office* →
Miss Lyons is going to the post office.

1 What are you wearing? *a gray suit*
2 Where are the students standing? *at the bus stop*
3 Who is buying the car? *Miss Gibbons*
4 What are you mailing? *two letters*
5 What is Mr. Thomas waiting for? *the bus*
6 Who is delivering the mail? *the letter carrier*
7 What are they carrying? *a picnic basket*

8   Who is speaking to the clerk?   *Mr. Harrison*
9   Where is the girl studying?   *in the bedroom*
10 Where are we going?   *to the bank*

Present progressive tense: ~~x~~–*ing*

A   Substitute.

The doctor is | closing the door.
driving a new car.
coming soon.
leaving soon.

I'm
They're
We're
He's | writing letters.

B   Answer.
Are you coming in?
Are you writing a book?
Is Mr. Lee driving to school today?
Is Mrs. Lee taking the train?
Is the train leaving soon?
Are the tellers taking the money?
Are they making the deposits?
Are we closing the store early today?
Are we taking the bus to the country?

A mail truck

speak   speak + ing   =   **speaking**

leave   leav~~e~~ + ing   =   **leaving**
come   com~~e~~ + ing   =   **coming**
write   writ~~e~~ + ing   =   **writing**

I am (I'm)
She is (She's)
He is (He's)
It is (It's)   coming.
You are (You're)   leaving.
We are (We're)
They are (They're)

We're leaving early today.
Miss Lyons is making a withdrawal.
Are the boys waking up?

Writing Practice

Follow the model.

Sometimes she makes a deposit. →
Is she making a deposit today?

1   Sometimes the bus leaves early.
2   Sometimes Mr. Lee drives the big car.
3   Sometimes he comes alone.
4   Sometimes I close the office early.
5   Sometimes the students write letters.
6   Sometimes she makes a withdrawal.
7   Sometimes we give the boy money.
8   Sometimes they drive a truck.

Present progressive tense: verbs like *to swim*

A Repeat.
Is the train stopping now?
I'm getting off now.
The boys are swimming in the lake.

B Answer.
Are the trains running late today?
Are the girls getting on the bus?
Are you putting the money in the drawer?
Are you beginning to work?
Am I swimming fast?
Are you putting the letters in the mailbox?
Is the truck stopping now?
Are you and the boys getting up now?

SUMMARY

speak	speak + ing	=	**speaking**
leave	leav̶e̶ + ing	=	**leaving**
put	put + t + ing	=	**putting**
run	run + n + ing	=	**running**
swim	swim + m + ing	=	**swimming**
stop	stop + p + ing	=	**stopping**

I am (I'm)
She is (She's)
He is (He's)
It is (It's) ——— rushing.
You are (You're) leaving.
We are (We're) stopping.
They are (They're)

The bus is stopping now.
The boy is beginning to walk.
We're getting off at Center Street.

Writing Practice

Follow the model.

> (get) Many people are _____ on the bus. →
> Many people are getting on the bus.

1 (stop) The truck is _____ near the bank.
2 (wash) Who is _____ the car?
3 (close) Mrs. Day is _____ the office.
4 (begin) We're _____ to deliver the mail.
5 (swim) The girls are _____ in the lake.
6 (run) The boys are _____ in the park.
7 (write) She's _____ a book.
8 (buy) Mr. and Mrs. Jenkins are _____ a new house.
9 (make) I'm _____ a withdrawal.
10 (put) Are you _____ the car in the garage?
11 (get) Are we _____ off now?
12 (hurry) Miss Lyons is _____ to the bank.

Mailing a package

CONVERSATION

At the post office

Woman Do I buy stamps here?

Clerk Yes, ma'am.

Woman OK. I need airmail stamps for a package and a letter—no, for two letters.

(The clerk gives the stamps to the woman.)

Woman Do I mail the package with the letters?

Clerk No. I take the package.

Woman Where do I mail the letters?

Clerk In the mailbox over there.

Woman Where?

Clerk Over there in the corner. See? A man is mailing a letter there now.

Woman Oh, yes, I see. Thank you.

Questions

1 Does the woman buy stamps here?
2 Does she need airmail stamps?
3 What is she mailing?
4 Does she mail the package with the letters?
5 Does the clerk have to take the package?
6 Where does she mail the letters?
7 Where is the mailbox?
8 Is a man mailing a letter there now?

Personal Questions

1 Do you go to the post office?
2 Do you mail letters there?
3 Do you buy stamps too?

4 Do you put letters in the mailbox?
5 Do you write letters to friends?
6 Do you send pictures to friends?

A busy day at the post office

It's a busy day at the post office. Letter carriers are leaving to deliver the mail. Customers are coming in and going out. Many people are standing in line. Some are buying stamps. Others are putting letters in the mailbox. One woman is writing a name and address on a package.

A man is waiting in line. He asks the clerk, "Where do I mail a large package?"

"Next window, please."

A woman in line asks, "I want to mail a letter to Peru. Do I buy the stamps here?"

"Yes, you do."

"I want to send the letter airmail. How many stamps do I need?"

"Three."

"Is the mail leaving soon?"

"Yes, they're putting the mail on the trucks now."

The woman puts the stamps on the envelope and gives the letter to the clerk.

There are still many people in line at each window. The clerks are having a busy morning. A new day is just beginning.

Questions

1 Is it a busy day at the post office?
2 Are letter carriers leaving to deliver the mail?
3 Are customers coming in and going out?
4 Are many people standing in line?
5 Are some buying stamps?
6 Are others putting letters in the mailbox?
7 Who is writing a name and address on a package?
8 Does the man have to go to the next window?
9 What does the woman want to buy?
10 How many airmail stamps does she need?
11 Is the mail leaving soon?
12 Are they putting the mail on the trucks now?
13 Does the woman put the stamps on the envelope and give the letter to the clerk?
14 Are there still many people in line at each window?
15 Are the clerks having a busy morning?
16 Is a new day just beginning?

"You need three stamps."

111

LESSON REVIEW

I Complete the sentences.

I write the name and _____ on the envelope. →
I write the name and address on the envelope.

sending	stamps	out
letter carrier	still	truck
package	name	deliver
soon	address	writing
mailbox	clerk	Each

1 He buys two _____ for the letter.
2 Mr. Harris is a _____. He delivers the mail.
3 The girl puts the mail in the _____ on the corner.
4 Do I mail the _____ with the letter?
5 The _____ is 24 Center Street, Oakland.
6 The _____ on the package is Miss Mary Rand.
7 They're _____ the package to Japan.
8 The mail is leaving soon. They are putting the mail on the _____ now.
9 Letter carriers _____ the mail.
10 Miss Carter is a _____ in the post office. She is at the next window.
11 I am not coming in; I am going _____.
12 _____ teller at the bank has a window.
13 The doctor is not here now. He is coming _____.
14 The customer is _____ the name and address on the package.
15 Where is Mr. Hart? Is he _____ working at the office?

II Answer the questions. Write a story.

Is it a busy day at the post office?
Are there many people in line at each window?
Are letter carriers leaving to deliver the mail?
Are customers coming in and going out?
Are they putting letters in the mailbox?
Are they buying stamps from the clerks?
Is the mail leaving soon?
Are they putting the mail on the trucks now?
Are the clerks having a busy day?
Is every day a busy day at the post office?

LESSON 8

NEW WORDS

1   Mrs. Louis has a restaurant.
She is the owner.
A man is sitting at a table.
He has a menu.
He is ready to order.
The service here is excellent.
The waiter brings an appetizer.
He waits on the customer.

2   The woman wants something to
        eat.
     She orders dinner.
     Dinner is a big meal.
     She asks for meat, vegetables,
        and a salad.
     She tells the waitress she wants
        dessert too.
     The waitresses are very busy.

3   The chef's special is fish.
     It is delicious.
     It is really good.
     It is superb.

4 After the meal, the waitress
      brings the check.
   The man pays the bill.
   He leaves a tip on the table.

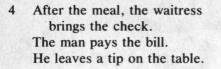

5 The Moores usually eat at
      home.
   They don't like to eat out.

food what you eat
        The food in the Louis restaurant is always good.

A Answer the questions.

   1 Who has a restaurant?
   2 Is she the owner?
   3 Who is sitting at a table?

4 What does he have?
5 Is he ready to order?
6 Is the service here excellent?
7 Who brings an appetizer?
8 What does the waiter bring?
9 Does he wait on the customer?
10 Does the woman want something to eat?
11 Does she order dinner?
12 What does she ask for?
13 Does she tell the waitress she wants dessert too?
14 Are the waitresses very busy?
15 What is the chef's special?
16 Is it delicious?
17 Is it superb?
18 When does the waitress bring the check?
19 Who pays the bill?
20 Does the man leave a tip on the table?
21 Where do the Moores usually eat?
22 Do they like to eat out?

B Complete the sentences.

1 The customer reads the _____ in the restaurant.
2 She pays the _____ and then leaves the restaurant.
3 I don't eat at _____; I always eat out.
4 They always leave a big _____ for the waitress.
5 I don't want meat. I'm having _____ today.
6 He likes to have _____ after a meal.
7 The food is really good. It's _____.
8 She waits on customers in a restaurant. She is a _____ there.

"Here is the check, sir."

MORE NEW WORDS

Sunday
Monday
Tuesday
Wednesday
Thursday
Friday
Saturday

bread

napkin

coffee

tea

cup

soup

STRUCTURE

Possessives

Singular nouns: *girl/girl's*

A Repeat.
The girl's mother is a teacher.
Mr. Platt's car is new.
The woman's coats are small.

B Substitute.

The teacher's
The doctor's | office is over there.
Mr. Dee's

Miss Gordon's
The owner's | keys are in the drawer.
The teller's

118

C **Answer.**
Does he want the chef's salad?
Do you have the teacher's books?
Is Mrs. Kent's hat new?
Are the waiter's tips on the table?
Is the woman's son a doctor?
Are you bringing the customer's dessert?
Is the teller's money in the drawer?
Is today's menu very good?

Plural nouns: *girls/girls'*

A **Repeat.**
I have the students' books.
The waiters' tips are on the table.
The tellers' money is in the drawer.

B **Substitute.**

	customers'	
The	boys'	meals are ready.
	teachers'	

	girls'	
She is bringing the	Stones'	check.
	doctors'	

C **Answer.**
Is the waitress bringing the customers' meals?
Are the boys' shirts new?
Are the customers' deposits in the bank?
Does the owner have the waiters' tips?
Are the teachers' books in the room?
Is the owners' friend in the restaurant?
Is the Stones' package in the mail?
Is the doctors' office here?

appetizers

California Tomato Juice ...... .50	Fresh Fruit Cup 1.00
Half Grapefruit .... .95	Gulf Shrimp Cocktail 3.25
Soup du Jour .... .95	Baked Clams Oreganato 1.75
Quiche Lorraine 1.25	Antipasto 1.50

salads

Chef's Salad Bowl 4.25
*Ham, turkey & swiss cheese on crisp
greens, tomatoes & olives.*

Jumbo Shrimp Platter 6.50
*Gulf shrimp, cole slaw, celery hearts,
tomato quarters, cocktail sauce.*

featured today

N.Y. Cut Sirloin Steak 8.25
Herb butter.

Chopped Beef Steak 4.25
sauteed mushrooms and onions.

Mushroom Omelette 4.50
Water Cress.

Deep Fried Gulf Shrimp 5.25
Cole Slaw—Tartar Sauce.

Filet of Sole 5.25
Lemon butter.

Boned Breast of Chicken 4.75
Brandied Cherry Sauce.

all entrees served with choice of vegetable or potato

French Fried Onion Rings . . .95
or Mushroom Caps 1.50

carving board

Roast Sirloin of Beef 3.75
Au Jus on rye.

Baked Virginia Ham 3.75
on rye.

Tuna Club African Queen 3.50
*White meat tuna salad, crisp
bacon, water cress, tomato.*

Princess Club 3.50
*Shrimp salad, swiss cheese
bacon, lettuce & tomato.*

Safari Club Special 3.50
*Tender ham, swiss cheese and
banana on black pumpernickel.*

Turkey Club 3.50
*Sliced turkey breast, bacon,
lettuce and tomato.*

Rueben Grill—Corned Beef, Sauerkraut & Swiss Cheese . . . 4.00

Beef Burger Deluxe

Jumbo Burger   *sesame seed roll with Safari potatoes* 2.75
. . *with cheddar cheese* 3.00

Swiss Cheese Burger   *tomato & swiss cheese* 3.75
above served with dill pickle and cole slaw

petite salads

Garden Salad Bowl 95
Cole Slaw 95

Hearts of Lettuce 95
Macaroni Salad 95

desserts & beverages

French Ice Cream 95
Creamy Rice Pudding 75
Hot Fudge Sundae 1.50
Apple Pie—a la mode
   or sharp cheddar 1.25

Amaretto Parfait 1.50
Pastry Cart 1.50
Baked Apple 1.50
Sherbet 75
Blueberry Pie 1.00

coffee · tea · milk · soft drink · sanka 50
espresso 60

SUMMARY

the **girl's** hat   the **boy's** magazine

the **girls'** hats   the **boys'** magazine

The man's house is very big.
The man's books are on the table.

The teacher has the students' books.
Are you the students' friend?

Writing Practice

Follow the models.

> boy / friend →
> the boy's friend
>
> teachers / books →
> the teachers' books

1 teller / money
2 waiters / tips
3 ' man / mother
4 doctors / cars
5 girls / mother
6 students / books
7 chef / name
8 restaurants / menus
9 customer / passbooks
10 hospital / address

Noun plurals: *buses*

A Repeat.
The buses are running late.
The waitresses are working.
The nurses are busy.

B Answer.
Are the buses crowded?
Are the mailboxes full?
Are the addresses in the book?
Are the waitresses leaving?

Are the offices open today?
Do you have the packages?
Are you calling the nurses?
Are the prices on the menu?
Are the houses here expensive?

SUMMARY

bus	package
buses	packages

The restaurant has many waitresses.
The nurses are coming soon.

Writing Practice

A Complete with the plural of the word.

(package) Mrs. Winston is mailing the _____. →
Mrs. Winston is mailing the packages.

1 (nurse) We're looking for the _____.
2 (office) Mr. Warren likes the new _____.
3 (mailbox) The _____ are empty.
4 (address) I don't have the names and _____ of the teachers.
5 (waitress) The _____ come in at five o'clock.
6 (house) There are two new _____ across the street.
7 (bus) The _____ leave at eight o'clock.

B Complete with the singular of the word.

> (houses) They live in an old ____. →
> They live in an old house.

1 (waitresses) Please call the ____.
2 (mailboxes) Is there a ____ on the corner?
3 (prices) What is the ____ of the car?
4 (packages) Give the ____ to the clerk.
5 (buses) Does the ____ to the city stop here?
6 (nurses) The doctor has a new ____.

Preposition *with*

A Repeat.
I'm going to the store with Miss Lyons.
Please mail the letter with the package.
Mr. Baker wants coffee with the meal.

B Answer.
Is the teacher going with the students?
Are you going to the country with a friend?
Do you work with many people?
Do you want tea with the meal?
Is the truck leaving with the mail?
Is she going to the post office with the package?
Do you pay with cash?
Are the napkins with the cups?

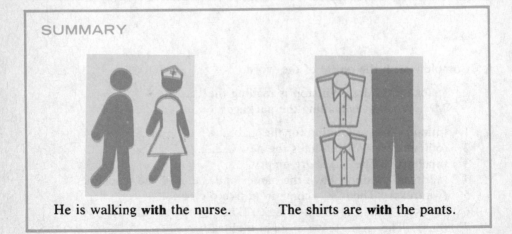

SUMMARY

He is walking **with** the nurse.   The shirts are **with** the pants.

Writing Practice

Make sentences. Use *with*.

boys / are / teacher →
The boys are with the teacher.

1 Mrs. Bush / is coming / Miss Lyons
2 teller / works / banker
3 jacket / is / pants
4 Mr. Carson / is driving / friend
5 letter carriers / are leaving / mail
6 shirt / is / suit
7 He / wants coffee / meal
8 waiter / is coming / food

CONVERSATION

At a restaurant

Mr. Kent	Waiter, bring the menu, please.
Waiter	Here it is, sir. Do you want to order now?
Mrs. Kent	Yes, we do. I'm having soup and fish.
Waiter	And you, sir?
Mr. Kent	Vegetables and meat, please.
Waiter	And a salad?
Mr. Kent	Yes. Two salads, please.
	(After the meal)
Mr. Kent	Waiter, the check, please.
Mrs. Kent	The service here is really excellent, and the prices aren't bad. Leave a nice tip for the waiter.

Questions

1. Does the waiter bring the menu?
2. Do Mr. and Mrs. Kent want to order now?
3. What is Mrs. Kent having?
4. What is Mr. Kent having?
5. Do they order two salads?
6. When do they ask for the check?
7. Is the service here really excellent?
8. Do they leave a nice tip for the waiter?

Personal Questions

1. Do you eat in a restaurant often?
2. Where is the restaurant?
3. Is the service always excellent?
4. Who usually brings the menu?
5. What do you have to eat?
6. Is the food always delicious?
7. When do you ask for the check?
8. Do you always leave a nice tip for the waiter (waitress)?

READING

Eating out

On Fridays Mr. and Mrs. Stone don't eat at home. They go out to eat. They usually like to go to a small restaurant near home. They like the food there, and the waiters and waitresses are good. The owner always has a corner table ready for the Stones.

They sit at the table. A waiter puts bread and napkins on the table. A waitress comes with the menu. She waits on the Stones. They order an appetizer. Then they begin to look at the menu.

"What's good on today's menu?" Mr. Stone asks the waitress.

"The chef's salad is the special today. It's superb."

"Fine. Bring the salad first and then coffee."

"And you, Mrs. Stone?"

"I'm having fish with vegetables today."

"Something for dessert?"

"No, just coffee after the meal."

The waitress brings the food and the Stones begin to eat. The meal is delicious. Mr. Stone says to the waitress, "Please tell the chef the salad is delicious."

126

After dinner, the Stones have a cup of coffee. Then they ask the waitress for the check.

"Bring the check, please."

The waitress brings the Stones' check. They pay the bill and leave a tip for the waitress.

Questions

1 When do Mr. and Mrs. Stone go out to eat?
2 Where do they usually like to go?
3 Does the owner always have a corner table ready?
4 What does the waiter put on the table?
5 Who comes with the menu?
6 Do the Stones order an appetizer first?
7 What is the special today?
8 What does Mr. Stone want to eat?
9 What is Mrs. Stone having today?
10 Are they having something for dessert?
11 Is the meal delicious?
12 What do they have after dinner?
13 Do they ask for the check?
14 Who brings the Stones' check?
15 Do they pay the bill?
16 Do they leave a tip for the waitress?

LESSON REVIEW

I Complete the sentences.

She leaves a _____ for the waitress. →
She leaves a tip for the waitress.

check	cup	waiter	service
waitress	menu	chef's	meal
After	waits on	superb	tells
appetizer	order		

1 The _____ works in a restaurant. She brings food to the customers.
2 The man always orders an _____ first.
3 A _____ works in a restaurant. He takes customers' orders.
4 The _____ salad is the special today.
5 The _____ in a small restaurant is usually excellent.
6 _____ the meal, they pay the bill and leave.
7 The waitress _____ the customer what is good on the menu.
8 The vegetables are very good. They are really _____.
9 Do you want a _____ of coffee after dinner?
10 A waiter or a waitress _____ customers in a restaurant.
11 They read the _____ to see what there is to eat today.
12 Call the waiter and ask for the _____ now. I am ready to leave.
13 Is breakfast always a big _____?
14 I always _____ soup first.

II Answer the questions. Write a story.

Do you like to eat out sometimes?
Do you always go to a nice restaurant?
Does the waitress (waiter) bring the menu?
Do you usually have an appetizer first?
What do you like to order?
Does the waitress (waiter) bring the food?
Is the food always delicious?
Do you have coffee with the meal? After the meal?
Do you have dessert too?
After the meal, do you pay the check?
Do you leave a big tip for the waitress (waiter)?

VOCABULARY _____

The number following each entry indicates the lesson in which the word first was first presented.

A

a 1
account 4
across 5
address 7
after (*prep.*) 8
again 4
airmail 7
alone 5
also 2
always 2
am 1
American 1
an 5
and 1
another 6
appetizer 8
are 1
aren't 5
ask 4
at 5

B

back 5
bad 8
bank 4
banker 1
bathroom 3
bedroom 3
begin 6
big 1
bill 8
blouse 7
book 2
boy 1
breakfast 6
bread 8
bring 8
building 5
bus 5
bus stop 5
busy 5
but 5
buy 2

C

call 2
car 2
carry 2
cash 4
catch 6
center 5
chair 3
change (*v.*) 6
check (*n.*) 4
checking account 4
chef 8
city 1
clerk 6
clock 5
close (*v.*) 6
coat 7
coffee 8
cold 5
come 5
corner 5
country 1
cross 6
crowded 5
cup 8
customer 4

D

daughter 3
day 2
delicious 8
deliver 6
deposit (*v.*) 4
deposit (*n.*) 4
deposit slip 4
dessert 8
dining room 3
dinner 8
do 7
doctor 1
doesn't 3
don't 3
door 3
downstairs 3
drawer 4

dress (*n.*) 7
dress (*v.*) 6
drive 2

E

each 7
early 6
eat 6
empty 5
English 2
envelope 7
every 2
excellent 8
expensive 3

F

family 3
fare 5
fast 6
father 3
find 3
fine 1
first 6
fish 8
food 8
for 5
for sale 3
Friday 8
friend 2
from 4
full 5

G

garage 3
get 5
get off 5
get on 5
get up 6
girl 1
give 4
go 2
good 8
good-bye 5
gray 5

H

happy 3
hat 7
have 3
have to 3
has 3
he 1
hello 1
help (*n.*) 4
help (*v.*) 4
here 2
he's 1
home 8
hospital 1
hot 2
house 1
how (*inter. pron.*) 1
how many? 3
how often? 5
hurry 2
husband 1

I

I 1
I'm 1
in 1
is 1
isn't 5
it (*subj. pron.*) 1
it's 1

J

jacket 7
just 6

K

key 3
kitchen 3

L

lake 2
large 4
late 6
lawyer 1
leave 2
letter 7

letter carrier 7
like 8
line 4
live 2
living room 3
long 6
look 4
look at 5

M

magazine 2
mail (*n.*) 7
mail (*v.*) 7
mailbox 7
make 4
man 1
many 3
meal 8
meat 8
meet 5
menu 8
minute 5
Miss 2
Monday 8
money 4
morning 3
mother 3
Mr. 1
Mrs. 1
much 4

N

name 7
napkin 8
near 3
need 4
neighborhood 3
new 3
newspaper 2
next (*adj.*) 7
nice 2
no 1
not 1
now 3
nurse 1

O

o'clock 5
of 2

off 5
office 5
office building 5
often 5
oh 1
old 3
on 5
open 5
or 1
order 8
others (*pron.*) 7
out 7
outside (*adv.*) 5
over there 6
owner 8

P

package 7
pants 7
park 3
passbook 4
pay (*v.*) 5
people 5
picnic basket 2
picture 2
platform 6
please 4
post office 7
price 3
push 6
put 4

Q

quiet 3

R

read 2
ready 5
really 8
realtor 3
restaurant 8
ride 6
room 3
run (bus) 5
rush (*v.*) 6
rush hour 5

1.	one	90.	ninety
2.	two	100.	one hundred
3.	three	101.	one hundred one
4.	four	120.	one hundred twenty
5.	five	125.	one hundred twenty-five
6.	six	200.	two hundred
7.	seven	500.	five hundred
8.	eight	1,000.	one thousand
9.	nine	1,001.	one thousand one
10.	ten	1,050.	one thousand fifty
11.	eleven	1,100.	one thousand one hundred
12.	twelve		(eleven hundred)
13.	thirteen	1,250.	one thousand two hundred fifty
14.	fourteen		(twelve hundred fifty)
15.	fifteen	5,000.	five thousand
16.	sixteen	10,000.	ten thousand
17.	seventeen	100,000.	one hundred thousand
18.	eighteen	1,000,000.	one million
19.	nineteen	1,000,000,000.	one billion
20.	twenty		
21.	twenty-one		
22.	twenty-two		
23.	twenty-three		
24.	twenty-four		
25.	twenty-five		
26.	twenty-six		
27.	twenty-seven		
28.	twenty-eight		
29.	twenty-nine		
30.	thirty		
40.	forty		
50.	fifty		
60.	sixty		
70.	seventy		
80.	eighty		

TIME

1:00	It's one o'clock.
2:00	It's two o'clock.
3:00	It's three o'clock.
4:00	It's four o'clock.
5:00	It's five o'clock.
6:00	It's six o'clock.
7:00	It's seven o'clock.
8:00	It's eight o'clock.
9:00	It's nine o'clock.
10:00	It's ten o'clock.
11:00	It's eleven o'clock.
12:00	It's twelve o'clock.
12:00 P.M.	It's noon.
12:00 A.M.	It's midnight.
1:00 A.M.	It's one o'clock in the morning.
1:00 P.M.	It's one o'clock in the afternoon.
2:15	It's two fifteen.
	It's a quarter after (past) two.
	It's fifteen minutes after (past) two.
3:30	It's three thirty.
	It's half past three.
3:45	It's three forty-five.
	It's a quarter to four.
	It's fifteen minutes to four.
4:20	It's four twenty.
	It's twenty minutes after (past) four.
4:35	It's four thirty-five.
	It's twenty-five (minutes) to five.

DAYS

Sunday	Tuesday	Thursday	Saturday
Monday	Wednesday	Friday	

MONTHS

January	April	July	October
February	May	August	November
March	June	September	December